A Practical Guide
to Library of
Congress Classification

For Reference

A Practical Guide to Library of Congress Classification

Karen Snow

ROWMAN & LITTLEFIELD

Lanham • Boulder • New York • London

Published by Rowman & Littlefield
A wholly owned subsidiary of
The Rowman & Littlefield Publishing Group, Inc.
4501 Forbes Boulevard, Suite 200, Lanham, Maryland 20706
www.rowman.com

Unit A, Whitacre Mews, 26-34 Stannary Street, London SE11 4AB

British Library Cataloguing in Publication Information Available

Library of Congress Cataloging-in-Publication Data Available

ISBN 9781538100660 (hardback : alk. paper) | ISBN 9781538100677 (pbk. :
alk. paper) | ISBN 9781538100684 (ebook)

∞™ The paper used in this publication meets the minimum requirements of
American National Standard for Information Sciences—Permanence of Paper
for Printed Library Materials, ANSI/NISO Z39.48-1992.

Printed in the United States of America

Contents

Preface

At first glance, library call numbers appear to be mysterious and random combinations of numbers and letters—an uncrackable code. Yet somehow these call numbers, whose foundations are formed primarily bỹ Library of Congress Classification (LCC) and Dewey Decimal Classification (DDC) in the United States, magically place resources on similar subjects together on the shelf. This categorization is not arbitrary at all, but quite intentional. The enigmatic codes do mean *something*: they primarily represent the subject matter of the work.

For as long as there have been libraries, there has been library classification: the system used to organize and arrange a physical collection, whether of books, magazines, DVDs, or any other item—even digital resources—benefits from classification systems. Some form of classification is necessary for the efficient functioning of a library with collections that can be openly browsed by users. Without a system for organizing a library collection, even the most carefully crafted catalog is rendered useless as users would need to scour the entire library to find the specific item they want. Even browsing is hampered, since most people browse with some general idea of what they're looking for, even if it's just fiction versus nonfiction.

Technically, assigning subject headings and subheadings is "classifying" as well, but modern classification systems not only provide subject collocation of works but also use some sort of notation to assist in the physical organization of library materials.

In other words, library classification systems serve two major purposes:

• They provide an "address" for each item.
• They group similar items together in a logical sequence.

Traditionally, library classification schemes have used number codes (Dewey Decimal) or letter/number codes (Library of Congress). However, the use of these specific notations, though common, is not essential; the type of notation you use (whether it is numbers, letters, or complete words or phrases) depends on the type of library user population you serve and the size of the collection.

This book is based on my LCC lectures from the beginning cataloging courses I teach. It is designed for library school students, new catalogers, accidental catalogers, and, quite frankly, anyone who needs and/or wants to understand and create LCC call numbers but does not want to wade through lots of cataloging jargon and extremely detailed explanations. I've tried to discuss LCC using easy-to-understand language and without assuming prior knowledge of cataloging principles and standards. I wrote this book with the goal of providing a solid foundation of LCC knowledge to my readers, not to cover every scenario one may encounter when creating LCC call numbers. With this is mind, I highly recommend consulting the main sources I use to explain the how and why of LCC call number construction: Classification Web and the *Classification and Shelflisting Manual* (CSM). They will provide further guidance as this book only scratches the surface of the complexities of LCC.

Most chapters of this book provide step-by-step instructions on how to construct an LCC call number, as well as practice exercises at the end of the chapter to test what you've learned. The answers to these exercises can be found in the "Answers to End-of-Chapter Exercises" appendix. As you move through the book, the exercises build on each other so that by the time you reach the end, you will be able to create full LCC call numbers on a variety of topics. I begin by explaining briefly the background of LCC and the main components of LCC call numbers. Before we start building LCC call numbers, I will discuss each part of the call number, particularly the meaning and construction of what are called "Cutter numbers," an important feature of LCC call number building. I will also make sure you know what you are looking at in

LCC itself before we start building call numbers—the LCC schedules can be very intimidating! Only then will I describe basic LCC call number building and then move to advanced building using various types of tables. Throughout I will use plenty of examples and explain what I am doing during each step in the process. I will conclude the book by discussing the basics of building call numbers for fiction works and provide alternate avenues and resources for finding and learning more about LCC classification. I hope that this book will provide a solid foundation on which you can build on your love and knowledge of Library of Congress Classification!

1

Library of Congress Classification in a Nutshell

The Library of Congress Classification (LCC) scheme was developed in the late nineteenth and early twentieth centuries. Heavily influenced by Charles Ammi Cutter and the Dewey Decimal Classification (DDC) System, LCC was created *specifically* for the Library of Congress, and many of its quirks can be traced back to that origin and purpose. It is most commonly found in academic libraries, but it is used in all types of libraries around the world. LCC is a hierarchical system (starting with broad topics and subarranging by narrower ones) that divides subjects into general classes—twenty-one in this case—which are represented by one or more alphabet letters:

A. General Works
B. Philosophy. Psychology. Religion
C. Auxiliary Sciences of History
D. History: General and Old World
E. History: America
F. History: America
G. Geography. Anthropology. Recreation
H. Social Sciences
J. Political Science
K. Law
L. Education
M. Music and Books on Music
N. Fine Arts
P. Language and Literature

Q. Science
R. Medicine
S. Agriculture
T. Technology
U. Military Science
V. Naval Science
Z. Bibliography. Library Science

Additional letters (subclasses) are used to narrow the scope: ML = literature on music and KFL = Louisiana law. The letters are not initials for anything; M = Music and T = Technology mostly by happenstance. Also, the class schedules (i.e., the notation, terminology, and instructions for each class) were independently developed by subject specialists in that field, so there isn't a lot of consistency between classes—each has its own internal structure and quirks. There is also no underlying philosophical system for LCC. It was designed by the Library of Congress in order to organize its collections in the most practical way possible. For this reason, the LCC evolves largely based on what is called *literary warrant*. In other words, the Library of Congress rarely adds to, deletes from, or modifies LCC unless there is a compelling reason from the literature it collects to do so.

After the alphabet letters, each class or subclass is further refined using numbers and (sometimes) decimals, Cutter numbers (I will explain more about these in a moment), and a year of publication.

Here is a visual of the components of an LCC call number for the book *Introduction to Information Science* by David Bawden and Lyn Robinson, published in 2012:

Anatomy of an LCC Call Number

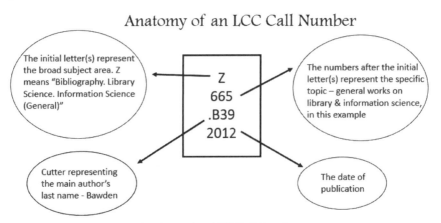

Anatomy of an LCC Call Number

Let's take a look at the elements that comprise an LCC call number. Each component will be discussed in greater depth in a later chapter, so don't fret if the following explanations aren't detailed enough!

CLASS NUMBER

LCC call numbers will always begin with one or more uppercase letters and one or more numbers following the letter(s). In most cases, this alphanumeric code will represent the main subject matter of the work. For example, instead of writing out that the resource is about the welfare of dogs, an LCC class number would use HV4746 to represent that concept.

HV4746 =
Welfare of dogs

CUTTERS

The next part of an LCC call number will be one or two "Cutters" (named after their creator, Charles Cutter). Cutters are also alphanumeric but are designed to organize an item alphabetically within a topic, usually by the main access point (i.e., the author's last name or the title of the book), but sometimes by geographic area or special topic as well. Cutters always begin with one uppercase letter and can contain one or more numbers after the initial letter. The first Cutter is preceded by a decimal point; if there is a second Cutter, it is preceded only by a space.

Cat = C38

Dog = D64

DATE

The last part of the LCC call number will usually be the year of publication, plus (in some cases) a "work letter" to differentiate between what would otherwise be identical call numbers.

Ideally, your goal should be to create a unique LCC call number for each item in the collection that will place the item in alphabetical order according to the main author of the work (or title if there is no main author).

The most common way to navigate LCC and build a call number is through Classification Web (http://classificationweb.net), produced by the Library of Congress. It does require a subscription, but it is completely online and allows you to search and browse

1974
1975
1976
1977
1978

Dates

LCC seamlessly. The screenshots you will see throughout this book are of LCC in Classification Web. You can also access LCC via portable document format (PDF) on the Library of Congress's website: https://www.loc.gov/aba/publications/FreeLCC/freelcc.html. The PDFs do not have the same functionality as Classification Web (for example, there are no hyperlinks that you can click on to access tables and other parts of LCC), nor are they updated as frequently as Classification Web, but they have the added benefit of being free to use! To demonstrate what I mean, here is a screenshot of a few entries in LCC subclass HB in Classification Web (I will explain what all this means in later chapters, so don't worry if you don't understand what you are seeing):

HB99.7	Keynesian economics
	Regional economics see HT388
	Environmental economics see HC79.E5
	By region or country
HB101	Austria Table H61
HB101.5	Czechoslovakia. Czech Republic Table H61
HB101.7	Slovakia Table H61
HB102	Hungary Table H61
HB103	Great Britain Table H61
HB104	Ireland Table H61
HB105	France Table H61

HB in Classification Web

And the same entries within the free PDFs (the class and subclasses, such as HB, are listed at the top of each page rather than with each number):

99.7	Keynesian economics
	Regional economics see HT388
	Environmental economics see HC79.E5
	By region or country
101	Austria (Table H61)
101.5	Czechoslovakia. Czech Republic (Table H61)
101.7	Slovakia (Table H61)
102	Hungary (Table H61)
103	Great Britain (Table H61)
104	Ireland (Table H61)
105	France (Table H61)

HB in PDFs

The Library of Congress no longer publishes LCC in print volumes, so if you want to create up-to-date call numbers, the two resources mentioned above are your best bet.

QUICK TIP . . .

The LCC call number is often based on the first subject heading listed in a catalog record, so if you already have subject headings, your work on the LC call number may be partially complete. In chapter 13 I discuss how to find LC class numbers using Library of Congress Subject Headings (LCSHs)!

The *Classification and Shelflisting Manual* (CSM), the Library of Congress's guide to LCC, is also available in PDF for free. As I mentioned previously, this resource is one of the main sources of information for this book, so I recommend consulting it if you need further guidance on a particular topic: https://www.loc.gov/aba/publications/FreeCSM/freecsm.html. It discusses the general principles of classification, filing rules, creating Cutters, as well as how to classify specific types of materials and topics, such as juvenile materials and government documents.

In the next few chapters I will examine each of the three parts of the call number more closely, starting with the end of the call number first (the date) and then working my way to the beginning (the class number).

EXERCISES

1. LCC has how many main classes?
2. What does the Library of Congress use to justify the creation, deletion, or modification of class numbers?
3. What are the three main parts of an LCC call number?
4. What is the name of the online, subscription-based resource produced by the Library of Congress that allows you to search and browse Library of Congress Classification?
5. What online resource is the Library of Congress's guide to LCC?

2

Dates

Let's look a bit more at the "date" part of the call number. There can only be one date per call number except for special cases (see below), and it will be the last part of the call number. It's usually pretty straightforward—when was the item published? That's your date! If your library uses the MARC (MAchine-Readable Cataloging) standard, you should use the date in the 264 field, second indicator "1," subfield $c. If there are multiple dates in the bibliographic record (like a publication and copyright date), that's OK. Choose the publication date. If the item uses Roman numerals, transcribe the date using Arabic numerals. For example, transcribe MMX as 2010.

In cases where the publication date is variable or unknown, use the following guidelines (the square brackets in some of the entries below indicate that the information is not on the resource itself but supplied by the cataloger):

Publication date	Date used in call number
[1970]	1970
[1976?]	1976
publication date = 1981 copyright date = ©1980	1981
[1962 or 1963]	1962
1979-1981	1979
[between 1977 and 1980]	1977
[not before May 1, 1960]	1960
[not after June 12, 1900]	1900

Date Guidelines

If you see "[date of publication not identified]" in the record, try your best to find another date (copyright, printing, distribution, etc.) that you can use in the call number. If there are additional characters such as square brackets and a question mark in the date of publication element, *do not* include these characters in the call number! Just put the year.

If you find yourself in a situation where you have multiple editions of the same work published in the same year, use lowercase letters starting with "b" to differentiate them (this is not as uncommon as you would think—sometimes a work will be published in different countries by different publishers). These lowercase letters are called "work letters" and help distinguish call numbers that would otherwise look exactly the same:

HV4746.S66 1982
(Original US edition)

HV4746.S66 1982b
(British edition, same date)

HV4746.S66 1982c
(Revised US edition, same date)

The work letter "a" is used for facsimile reprints and photocopies. Add "a" to the end of the publication date of the original item's call number:

GV1449.5.J66 1960
(Original edition)

GV1449.5.J66 1960a
(Facsimile reprint)

If you are cataloging a multipart item, use the date associated with the earliest or first part:

SF427.45.R56 1990
(Item published from 1990 until 2003)

In some cases, LCC will call for two dates in a single call number. For example, assume you are cataloging the following title:

The Olympics of 1972: A Munich Diary by Richard D. Mandell, published 1991

GV721.9	Facilities ⬭
GV721.92	Olympic torch ⬭
GV722	Individual contests. By year ⬭
	Subarrange by author
GV722.5.A-Z	Other contests and events, A-Z ⬭

Two Dates in a Call Number

The above is a screenshot of LCC within Classification Web (which we will talk more about shortly). Note the highlighted class number says to organize "By year" and then "Subarrange by author." If we follow these directions, our call number will look like this:

GV722 1972 .M35 1991

Before the 1980s, the Library of Congress rarely added the publication date to call numbers, but now it is standard practice. Being able to see the publication date within the call number can be very helpful when browsing the shelves; one can instantly distinguish between newer and older publications.

EXERCISES

1. The item you are cataloging was published in 1981. What year should you include in the call number for this work?
2. The item you are cataloging was published in 2001, with a copyright date of 2000. What year should you include in the call number for this work?
3. You think the item you are cataloging was published in 1959, but it is questionable. In 264_1$c you put [1959?]. How should you transcribe the date in the call number for this item?
4. You are cataloging a facsimile reprint of an item that originally was published in 1923. How should you transcribe the date in the call number for this item?
5. You are cataloging two editions of the same work published in the same year: 2015. You assign the following call number to one of the editions: NK1170 .B45 2015. What call number should you assign to the other edition to distinguish it from the first?

6. You are cataloging an item that you think was published between 1968 and 1974. How should you transcribe the date in the call number for this item?

7. You are cataloging an item that was published in either 2001 or 2002. How should you transcribe the date in the call number for this item?

3

Cutter Numbers: What Are They?

Cutter numbers (or just "Cutters") are alphanumeric codes representing words or names that allow for the alphabetical arrangement of books on the shelf. They are placed after the classification number within the call number. They are a very important part of an LCC call number—in the vast majority of LCC call numbers, you will have at least one Cutter and sometimes two (but never more than two). They were invented by Charles Ammi Cutter in the late nineteenth century. He designed them to be used with his Expansive Classification System, which is not commonly used today, but his "Cutter numbers" have lived on. Cutters are used in both the Dewey Decimal Classification System and the Library of Congress Classification System. However, the Library of Congress uses its own Cutter table, and that is what we will be using in this book.

You might be wondering, if their purpose is alphabetization, why not use the first few letters of the author's last name (or of the title, or whatever you're using to alphabetize)? For smaller collections, you could do just that (and many libraries do!). For example, you might have seen the following on spine labels:

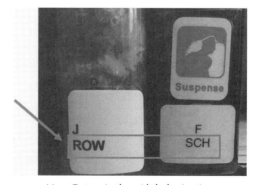

Non-Cutter Author Alphabetization

11

However, the Library of Congress Classification System was created by one of the largest libraries in the world, and when you have a large library, it's not at all uncommon to have, say, fifteen different books on the history of film by authors named Smith (not to mention Smithy, Smithson, Smithers . . . !). Clearly, there needs to be a better way to alphabetize large collections, and that's where Cutter numbers come in.

Here are some LCC call numbers with Cutters (surrounded by rectangles):

LCC Cutters

Each of these call numbers represents a work on the same topic (Z665) but by different authors (represented by the Cutters .F76, .G547, and .L89).

QUICK TIP . . .

At some libraries, nonfiction works are classified using LCC or Dewey, but fiction is organized by genre and then by the first three letters of the author's last name.

There are three main types of Cutters in LCC, and multiple types can be found in an LCC call number:

- Main entry—usually the last name of the author (or first-listed author) of the work (in the MARC 1XX field of a bibliographic record) or title if there is not an author main entry (e.g., Taylor = .T39).
- Cutters from the LC schedules or tables—can represent different things, like a topic, geographic place, a format, or time period (for

example, using .A2 for periodicals on a certain subject or .C5 for chocolate).
- Geographic Cutters—predetermined Cutters that represent a specific city, county, region, country, and so on (for example, Mexico = .M6).

Cutter numbers take the following form:

[alphabet letter] [one or more numbers]

for example:

Y77
W5
R5677892

How long they should be depends on the situation, but most "main entry Cutters" created to represent the main author of the work will be two numbers past the initial letter. There can be one or two Cutters per call number. If there are two Cutters in a call number, the first Cutter will have a period in front of it, but the second Cutter will not.

Main entry Cutters help keep works in alphabetical order by author's last name on the shelf within a specific subject area. So, for example, if you have five books in the class HC27 by authors Tabor, Taylor, Thorn, Tripp, and Tudor, their Cutters should be, respectively, .T33, .T39, .T56, .T75, and .T83. This ensures that when these books are placed on the shelf, they will be placed with Tabor's book first and Tudor's book last.

A work by Ethan Tabor	A work by Betty Taylor	A work by Anna Thorn	A work by George Tripp	A work by Sally Tudor
HC	HC	HC	HC	HC
27	27	27	27	27
.T33	.T39	.T56	.T75	.T83
2002	1999	1976	1996	1983

Examples of LCC Call Numbers

At this point, you are not expected to understand how I constructed .T39 from Taylor; we will talk about how to construct main entry Cutters in the next chapter.

There are a number of different Cutter tables—a general one that is used in most circumstances and several special tables that are used in specific situations, such as the Artists Table, the Translation Table, or the Biography Table. I will talk about a few of these later, but right now let's take a look at the basic LCC Cutter table:

1. After initial vowels								
for the second letter:	b	d	l-m	n	p	r	s-t	u-y
use the number-------→	2	3	4	5	6	7	8	9
2. After the initial letter S								
for the second letter:	a	ch	e	h-i	m-p	t	u	w-z
use the number-------→	2	3	4	5	6	7	8	9
3. After the initial letters Qu								
for the second letter:	a	e	i	o	r	t	y	
use the numbers-----→	3	4	5	6	7	8	9	
For the initial letters **Qa-QT**								
Use: **2-29**								
4. After other Initial consonants								
for the second letter:	a	e	i	o	r	u	y	
use the number ------→	3	4	5	6	7	8	9	
5. For expansion to an additional number								
for the next letter:	a-d	e-h	i-l	m-o	p-s	t-v	w-z	
use the number-------→	3	4	5	6	7	8	9	

LCC Cutter Table

We will go over what all this means in a moment, but a few things to keep in mind first:

1. Most main entry Cutter numbers are three characters long (i.e., .W54). Anything more or less than that is typically only done in special situations or to fit the number in a shelflist—more on that later. If you have to create another type of Cutter (like a place name or title), two characters long is usually sufficient.
2. Main entry Cutters never end with a zero or a one.
3. There can never be more than two Cutters per call number—if you have three or more Cutters, then you have done something wrong!

4

Creating a Main Entry Cutter Number

Now that you have a basic understanding of what a main entry Cutter number is and what it allows you to accomplish, let's practice creating Cutters. A reminder: the main entry Cutter represents the last name of the main author (or the first-listed author if there are multiple authors) or the title of the work if there is no main author.

Let's say you're Cuttering (yes, it can be verbed!) the name Addams. The first letter of the name is an "A," so you would start the Cutter with a decimal point (assuming it is the first Cutter in the call number) and the capital letter A:

.A

From here on out, you will be converting the remaining letters in Addams to numbers. As mentioned previously, main entry Cutters are usually two numbers past the initial letter, so that is what we will do here. The Cutter number for the second letter of the author's name depends on what the first letter is—whether it's a vowel, an "S," a "Q," or some other consonant. Addams starts with a vowel ("A"), so next you should look at line 1 of the table, titled "after initial vowels." The second letter in Addams is "d"; looking under "d" in the table, you'll find the number "3," so put that after the .A:

.A3

1. After initial **vowels**								
for the second letter:	b	d	l-m	n	p	r	s-t	u-y
use the number-------→	2	3	4	5	6	7	8	9

2. After the initial letter **S**								
for the second letter:	a	ch	e	h-i	m-p	t	u	w-z
use the number-------→	2	3	4	5	6	7	8	9

3. After the initial letters **Qu**							
for the second letter:	a	e	i	o	r	t	y
use the numbers-----→	3	4	5	6	7	8	9
For the initial letters **Qa-QT** Use: **2-29**							

4. After other **Initial consonants**							
for the second letter:	a	e	i	o	r	u	y
use the number ------→	3	4	5	6	7	8	9

5. For **expansion** to an additional number							
for the next letter:	a-d	e-h	i-l	m-o	p-s	t-v	w-z
use the number-------→	3	4	5	6	7	8	9

LCC Cutter Table—Line 1 Highlighted

Any additional numbers are called "expansions"—they extend the Cutter to allow further fine-tuning of the shelflist order. Usual practice is to extend Cutters two places past the initial letter unless otherwise instructed, so let's add an expansion number by consulting line 5. The third letter in Addams is "d" again. If we look under the "d" on line 5 of the table, we find the number "3" (note that this time, "3" corresponds to letters "a" through "d").

Addams = .A33

1. After initial **vowels**								
for the second letter:	b	d	l-m	n	p	r	s-t	u-y
use the number-------→	2	3	4	5	6	7	8	9

2. After the initial letter **S**								
for the second letter:	a	ch	e	h-i	m-p	t	u	w-z
use the number-------→	2	3	4	5	6	7	8	9

3. After the initial letters **Qu**							
for the second letter:	a	e	i	o	r	t	y
use the numbers-----→	3	4	5	6	7	8	9
For the initial letters **Qa-QT** Use: **2-29**							

4. After other **Initial consonants**							
for the second letter:	a	e	i	o	r	u	y
use the number ------→	3	4	5	6	7	8	9

5. For **expansion** to an additional number							
for the next letter:	a-d	e-h	i-l	m-o	p-s	t-v	w-z
use the number-------→	3	4	5	6	7	8	9

LCC Cutter Table—Line 5 Highlighted

Here are some additional examples:

Smith (starting with line 2)
S = initial letter = S
m = second letter after initial letter "s" (from line 2) = 6
i = expansion letter from line 5 = 5
Cutter = .S65 (don't forget the decimal point!)

Quimbly (starting with line 3)
Qu = initial letter (Qu counts together as Q) = Q
i = second letter after initial letters "Qu" (from line 2) = 5
m = expansion letter from line 5 = 6
Cutter = .Q56

Morales (starting with line 4)
M = initial letter = M
o = second letter after initial consonant (from line 4) = 6
r = expansion letter from line 5 = 7
Cutter = .M67

That is all well and good, but you may be wondering, what if the second and/or third letter of the name or title is *not* on the Cutter table, as in the name "Acker"? We will use line 1 because "A" is a vowel, but "c" is nowhere to be seen on line 1! What should you do? At this point it is helpful to keep in mind that the Cutter table is meant to be a guide and not a strict set of instructions. Remember, your ultimate goal in LCC call number creation is to create a unique call number that places the work in the proper order on *your* library's shelves. As long as the call number you create helps you meet this goal, you can fudge the numbers a little bit. Since "c" is between "b" and "d" on line 1, you can choose 2 or 3—either one is fine as long as it ensures that the call number is unique, keeps the works in alphabetical order on the shelf, and allows room for future additions to the collection.

Acker
A = initial letter = A
c = second letter after initial vowel (choosing "b") = 2
k = expansion letter = 5
Cutter = .A25

Additionally, if a letter is closer to one letter than another, as in the case of "Aker" (note that "k" is closer alphabetically to "l–m" than it is to "d" on line 1), then it is best to choose the closer letter or range of letters.

Aker
A = initial letter = A
k = second letter after initial vowel ("k" is closer to "l–m") = 4
e = expansion letter = 4
Cutter = .A44

QUICK TIP . . .

It may seem odd that there is so much flexibility built into the Cutter table, but it really is a *good* thing. This flexibility allows you to choose a Cutter that keeps your institution's resources in order on the shelf, which in turns makes it easier for users to find what they are looking for. The vast majority of users have no clue about Cutters, so don't worry too much about whether or not your Cutter is "right" or "wrong" as long as it makes sense on the shelf!

Some additional tips:

Ignore any punctuation marks or spaces if any exist in a name or title and Cutter abbreviations as they appear.

D'Ambrosio
D = initial letter = D
A = second letter after initial consonant = 3
m = expansion letter = 6
Cutter = .D36

St. Valentine
S = initial letter = S
t = second letter after initial consonant = 7
V = expansion letter = 8
Cutter = .S78

If you Cutter a title and it begins with an initial article such as *a*, *an*, or *the* (including initial articles in other languages), start Cuttering after the initial article.

The Panda's Thumb
P = initial letter = P
a = second letter after initial consonant = 3
n = expansion letter = 6
Cutter = .P36

Los Jardines ("Los" is an initial article in Spanish)
J = initial letter = J
a = second letter after initial consonant = 3
r = expansion letter = 7
Cutter = .J37

However, if the initial article is part of a personal or place name, *do not* ignore it.

Los Angeles (a place name)
L = initial letter = L
o = second letter after initial consonant = 6
s = expansion letter = 7
Cutter = .L67

El Greco (a personal name)
E = initial letter = E
l = second letter after initial vowel = 4
G = expansion letter = 4
Cutter = .E44

If a name is less than three letters long, Cutter out as far as you can. If the first word of a title contains less than three letters, keep Cuttering into the next word.

Li
L = initial letter = L
i = second letter after initial consonant = 5
Cutter = .L5

In the Clear
I = initial letter = I
n = second letter after initial vowel = 5
t = expansion letter = 8
Cutter = .I58

Names that begin with "Mc" and "Mac" should not be Cuttered the same—Cutter them as they appear.

McCarthy
M = initial letter = M
c = second letter after initial consonant = 4
C = expansion letter = 3
Cutter = .M43

MacCarthy
M = initial letter = M
a = second letter after initial consonant = 3
c = expansion letter = 3
Cutter = .M33

If a name or title begins with a Roman or Arabic numeral, assign a Cutter between .A12 and .A19, a range of Cutters that has been reserved for numbers. This ensures that names and titles that begin with a number will file first alphabetically. Let's say you are cataloging the following resources that have a title main entry and are located within the same class number:

1 Is the Loneliest Number
8 Mile
10 Things I Hate about You

We don't need to consult the Cutter table. Instead, use your judgment to assign a Cutter to each that will ensure that they stay in numerical order on the shelf, but also allowing for future additions to the collection (I will talk more about this in the next chapter on shelflisting).

.A13—*1 Is the Loneliest Number*
.A15—*8 Mile*
.A16—*10 Things I Hate about You*

By assigning the first title the Cutter .A13, I am "saving" .A12 for future additions to the collection. Cutters .A17 through .A19 can be used for later additions as well.

It is important to understand how to create a Cutter using the LCC Cutter table, but there is another, free resource currently available on the web that makes Cuttering a breeze. It is called the Cataloging Calculator by Kyle Banerjee. Here is the URL: http://calculate.alptown.com. Click on the LC Cutter radial button, type in the name or title you want to Cutter, and a Cutter is immediately generated on your screen.

The heavy use of Cutter numbers is one of the main features of LCC that distinguishes it from other classification schemes. Using these alphanumeric notations keeps the LCC call number more compact while also ensuring that no two resources will have the same call number. This uniqueness makes it easier to keep resources organized on the shelf.

EXERCISE

Cutter the following names and titles two digits past the initial letter (if applicable).

1. Issa
2. Willis
3. Takachi
4. Anwar
5. Florez
6. Kyrios
7. Simpson
8. Montgomery
9. MacKenna
10. De Souza
11. Ahrens
12. Chase
13. Ko
14. O'Connell
15. Schmidt
16. *Reference and Information Services*
17. *It's All in Your Head*
18. *Stretching*
19. *The Trickster*
20. *On My Own Two Feet*
21. *The Checklist Manifesto*
22. *Quest for the Selby Mirror*

5

Cutters and the Shelflist

The "shelflist" is another word for the inventory of a library's resources as they are ordered on the library's shelves. The Library of Congress's shelflist is, by necessity, different from your local public library's shelflist because each library has different resources in its collection, even though there will likely be some overlap.

Shelf of Books with LCC Call Numbers

The purpose of Cutter numbers is to arrange items alphabetically, so your final consideration when building a Cutter should always be how it will fit in your library's shelflist. If you Cutter "James Cooper" as .C66, but your library already has a work on the same topic by "Aaron Cooper" using .C66, you'll have to tweak the Cutter a bit. How much you tweak depends on the situation. Remember when I said that the LCC Cutter table should be used as a set of guidelines rather than strict instructions? Well, you are about to put your judgment to the test in this chapter!

Let's go back to our "James Cooper" and "Aaron Cooper" example. One way to resolve this conflict is simply to bump up the second number in James Cooper's Cutter by one digit, like this:

Information Science Primer by Aaron Cooper	*Introduction to Information Science* by James Cooper
Z 665 .C66 2010	Z 665 .C67 2015

LCC Call Numbers—Cooper

The general rule of thumb is to alphabetize names by the last name first, and if the last names are the same, organize by the first name. Because "James" comes after "Aaron" alphabetically, use .C67 for James Cooper so that James's book is shelved after Aaron's on the shelf, assuming .C67 is not already in use. Once again, .C67 does not adhere strictly to the LCC Cutter table, but that's OK—it keeps our shelflist in order and the call numbers different beyond just the publication date.

There is another way we can change James Cooper's Cutter to make it different from Aaron's, but first keep in mind two things: (1) Cutters can be expanded past two numbers, and (2) Cutters are ordered first by the initial letter and then as decimal numbers. This helps inform the second way we can approach the Aaron/James conundrum: by adding a number to .C66 to represent James Cooper, like this:

Information Science Primer by Aaron Cooper	*Introduction to Information Science* by James Cooper
Z 665 **.C66** 2010	Z 665 **.C667** 2015

LCC Call Numbers—Cooper

What I have done here is Cutter "Cooper" three digits past the initial letter rather than two digits. This is perfectly valid; it creates a different Cutter from Aaron Cooper's existing one, and it keeps James Cooper's book on the shelf after Aaron's (this assumes that .C667 is not already in use). Cutters can be expanded as far as needed in order to ensure an orderly shelflist. How long and complex a Cutter may become really depends on how many works you have on a particular topic. It is more likely that you will have to create modified and/or lengthy Cutters if you have one thousand titles on a specific topic than if you have just two or three titles.

To take things a step further, let's play around with the following theoretical shelflist. Pretend that these titles are already in your collection:

Information Science Primer by Aaron Cooper	Information Science by Michelle Cooper	Essential Information Science by Tim Corley	Information Science Manual by John Cosby	Information Science Fun Time by Sue Cotton
Z 665 **.C66** 2010	Z 665 **.C665** 1999	Z 665 **.C67** 2016	Z 665 **.C6723** 2001	Z 665 **.C68** 2011

LCC Call Number Shelflist

Even though "665" is a larger number than "67," because we are organizing decimal numbers, .C665 will always come before .C67. If math is not your forte (I feel your pain!), then look at each number a column at a time:

.C6<u>6</u>
.C6<u>6</u>5
.C6<u>7</u>
.C6<u>7</u>23
.C6<u>8</u>

All have a "6" immediately after the initial letter; then the numbers are organized numerically by the second number, the third number, and so forth.

Let's say you receive James Cooper's *Introduction to Information Science* and you need to fit it between Aaron Cooper's book and Michelle Cooper's book. If we choose .C67 like we did in our first option above, that will conflict with Tim Corley's Cutter. If you choose .C667, that will place James Cooper's book after Michelle Cooper's book. We want to choose a Cutter that will put James's book between Aaron's and Michelle's. There's no exact "right" answer, but it's a good idea to leave yourself some wiggle room for future additions to the collection, so a good candidate might be .C663.

You can extend Cutters as far as you need to in order to make something fit. You can also fudge the numbers a bit if your shelflist is way off from the basic Cutter table, but obviously it's a good idea to maintain your shelflist in such a way that you shouldn't need to resort to such measures. Regardless, a Cutter that is "correct" according to the table but that misalphabetizes an item on your shelf is *not* a correct number!

QUICK TIP . . .

At some institutions, catalogers will check the Library of Congress's catalog to see how well LC's call numbers match up to their local shelflist. This can be particularly useful if your institution performs a lot of copy cataloging (using records created by catalogers outside of your institution) because many catalogers will create call numbers with LC's shelflist in mind.

Another potential Cuttering problem can occur when you have two works by the same author on the same topic. If you have two call numbers that look like this, the assumption is that the work with the second call number is a newer edition of the work with the first call number:

Information Science Primer by Aaron Cooper	*Information Science Primer* by Aaron Cooper 2nd edition
Z 665 **.C66** 2010	Z 665 **.C66** 2015

LCC Call Number—Editions

In the above case, it is fine to use the same Cutter. The different years tell us that these are the same work but different editions. However, if an author wrote different works on the same topic (not simply different editions), then you need to adjust the Cutters of each work so it is clear they are different works. For example:

Information Science Primer by Aaron Cooper	*Information Science Through the Years* by Aaron Cooper
Z 665 **.C66** 2010	Z 665 **.C667** 2016

LCC Call Number—Same Author, Different Work

It is unlikely that you will need to spend too much time messing with Cutters for most items, but it is important to always check your shelflist before you assign a call number, just in case. The same can be said for copy cataloging—when you copy records from an outside source into your local system. Just because a call number fits nicely within the library shelflist of the person who created the call number originally does not mean that it will fit nicely into your library's shelflist!

EXERCISES

1. Assume that the authors in the following list have written works on the same topic. Cutter the names in a way that will ensure that they will be in alphabetical order within a shelflist.

   Salmon
   Sanchez
   Santos
   Saxton

Schofield
Schott
Shah
Short
Silva
Simmons
Singh

2. Assume that the authors in the following list have written works on the same topic. The first two in the list are titles on the same topic. Cutter the names and titles in a way that will ensure that they will be in alphabetical order within a shelflist. If you don't remember what to do with titles that begin with a number, review the last chapter!

3 in a Row (title main entry)
7 Winds Blow (title main entry)
Aaaaa, Bill
Ababa, Pam
Acton, Jill
Adams, Cynthia
Adams, Kathy
Adams, Michael
Adams, Nancy
Aglow, Thomas
Alfalfa, Charles

6

LCC in Classification Web

First, a reminder: Classification Web is an online, subscription-based resource created by the Library of Congress. It is a searchable and browse-able repository for Library of Congress Subject Headings, genre/form terms, and much more. It is also where you can find an interactive version of the Library of Congress Classification schedules with hyperlinks. If you recall, you can also access LCC for free on the Library of Congress's website (https://www.loc.gov/aba/publications/FreeLCC/freelcc.html—make sure you click on the "texts" and not the "outlines" if you want to see call number building instructions). It is fine to use either resource, but to keep things simple, I decided to stick with explaining LCC and using screenshots from Classification Web only rather than including explanations and screenshots from both Classification Web and the PDFs. Those of you who are using the PDFs only can skip the parts where I discuss searching and browsing in Classification Web. The remaining chapters should be applicable (with some minor adjustments) to both resources.

Next, this may seem counterintuitive, but I want to introduce you to what you will see in LCC before I explain how to get there. I promise it will make it easier for you (and me!) to explore the ins and outs of searching and browsing LCC in Classification Web. These entries will look the same in the free PDFs except for the hyperlinked items.

This is a typical screen in Classification Web within the TX schedule (Home economics—which includes cooking and baking), with class numbers on the left and what are called "captions" on the right:

	Cakes ▭
	Including cupcakes
TX771	General works ▭
TX771.2	Cake decorating ▭
TX771.4	Cake pops ▭
	Cheesecake see TX773 ▭
TX772	Cookies ▭
TX773	Desserts, pies, and puddings. Pastry ▭
	Including cheesecake
TX775	Directories of bakers, etc. ▭
TX776	Bakers' trade publications ▭
TX778	Bakers' and confectioners' supplies ▭
	Including catalogs
	Cf. TX657.B34 Baking pans ▭
	Confectionery ▭
	Periodicals see TX761 ▭
TX783	General works ▭
	Candy ▭
TX784	History of candy manufacture ▭
TX791	General works ▭

TX—Cooking and Baking

Captions present the meaning of the class number using English words. For example, TX772 is associated with the caption "Cookies." I added lines to the screenshot above to give you a clearer sense of which class numbers go to which caption:

	Cakes ▭
	Including cupcakes
TX771 ———————	General works ▭
TX771.2 ———————	Cake decorating ▭
TX771.4 ———————	Cake pops ▭
	Cheesecake see TX773 ▭
TX772 ———————	Cookies ▭
TX773 ———————	Desserts, pies, and puddings. Pastry ▭
	Including cheesecake
TX775 ———————	Directories of bakers, etc. ▭
TX776 ———————	Bakers' trade publications ▭
TX778 ———————	Bakers' and confectioners' supplies ▭
	Including catalogs
	Cf. TX657.B34 Baking pans ▭
	Confectionery ▭
	Periodicals see TX761 ▭
TX783 ———————	General works ▭
	Candy ▭
TX784 ———————	History of candy manufacture ▭
TX791 ———————	General works ▭

TX—Cooking and Baking with Horizontal Lines

Sometimes LCC includes notes like "Including cupcakes" under the caption "Cakes" to make it clear if a subcategory should be included. Also, take note of the line under "Bakers' and confectioners' supplies": Cf. TX657.B34 Baking pans. "Cf." is an abbreviation of the Latin verb *conferre*, which means literally "to bring together," but in English it means "compare." In this context, the Library of Congress is saying, compare TX778 ("Bakers' and confectioners' supplies") to a similar, yet different, class number, "TX657.B34 Baking pans." If you are familiar with Library of Congress Subject Headings (LCSH), the use of "Cf." is similar to the use of "see also" and "related terms." One of the many benefits of using Classification Web is that it hyperlinks "Cf." notes and "see" references (such as the "Cheesecake see TX773" and "Periodicals see TX761" you see above) so that you can click on the class number and find yourself magically transported to that part of the LCC schedules.

Also observe that some captions are more indented than others. Indented captions are more specific categories under the broader topic. For example, under "Cakes" you can choose TX771 (General works), TX771.2 (Cake decorating), and TX771.4 (Cake pops). "Cakes" does not have a class number associated with it because you cannot simply choose the topic "Cakes" in this instance—you have to specify if your work is a general work about baking cakes (TX771), a work on cake decorating (TX771.2), or a work on cake pops (TX771.4).

Even though it is sometimes difficult to do so visually, it is important to understand where a caption is located in the hierarchy. For example, the "General works" caption under "Cakes" (TX771) is specific to works on baking cakes as opposed to the "General works" under "Confectionery" (TX783), which should be applied to works about confectionery.

	Cakes
	Including cupcakes
TX771	General works
TX771.2	Cake decorating
TX771.4	Cake pops
	Cheesecake see TX773
TX772	Cookies
TX773	Desserts, pies, and puddings. Pastry
	Including cheesecake
TX775	Directories of bakers, etc.
TX776	Bakers' trade publications
TX778	Bakers' and confectioners' supplies
	Including catalogs
	Cf. TX657.B34 Baking pans
	Confectionery
	Periodicals see TX761
TX783	General works
	Candy
TX784	History of candy manufacture
TX791	General works

TX Hierarchy

Let's look at a different type of entry in LCC—one that includes Cutters that represent topics:

	Baking. Confectionery
	Cf. GT5960.B34-.B342 Manners and customs
TX761	Periodicals, societies, etc.
TX763	General works
TX765	Minor works, recipe books, etc.
TX767.A-Z	Recipes for special food products, A-Z
TX767.A65	Apple butter
TX767.C37	Caramel
TX767.C5	Chocolate
TX767.H7	Honey
TX767.M3	Maple sugar and syrup
TX767.W48	White chocolate
	Bread
TX769	General works
TX770.A-Z	Special breads, A-Z
TX770.B35	Bagels
TX770.B55	Biscuits. Scones
TX770.C45	Challah
TX770.C64	Corn bread

LC Class Numbers with Cutters

If you recall from our earlier discussion, there are many different types of Cutters. In chapter 4, we discussed how to create a main entry Cutter that represents the main author of a work or a title. But there are also Cutters used throughout LCC that represent a specific topic or format that you include *in addition to* the main entry Cutter (we will discuss this further when we start building LCC call numbers in chapter 9). The captions will make it clear when it is appropriate to include these types of Cutters.

Take a look at the captions that end with "A–Z" in the above screenshot (such as "Recipes for special food products, A–Z" and "Special breads, A–Z"). The class numbers associated with these captions also have "A–Z" (TX767.A–Z and TX770.A–Z). This does *not* mean that you add A–Z after the class number. The "A–Z" is a placeholder for the first Cutter, which should fit alphabetically between A and Z. For example, all of the special food products at TX767 have Cutters assigned to them that are alphabetically between A and Z: .A65 (Apple butter), .C37 (Caramel), .C5 (Chocolate), and so forth. I used vertical lines in the screenshot below to highlight the different levels of hierarchy.

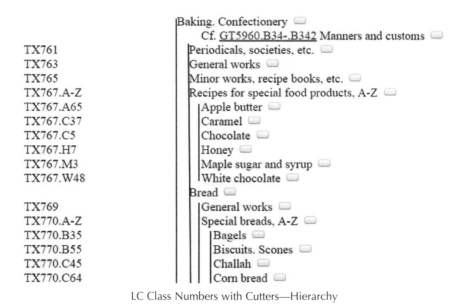

LC Class Numbers with Cutters—Hierarchy

It is important to include these Cutter numbers when building a call number because they narrow the focus of the class number; for example, TX767 should not be used unless you include the Cutter for the special food product immediately after it. Sometimes the Cutters are formulated strictly according to the LCC Cutter table, but sometimes they are not, so don't let that confuse you. Understanding what you are seeing in LCC takes time and practice, but it is an important step in learning how to build an LCC call number.

EXERCISES

Use this entry for TR721 through TR729 in Classification Web to answer the following questions:

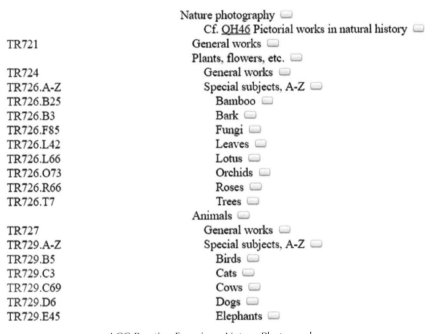

LCC Practice Exercise—Nature Photography

1. What three captions are the next step down hierarchically (indented the least) under "Nature photography"?
2. What class number should you assign a general work on the nature photography of flowers?
3. What other class number does LCC compare to "Nature photography"?

4. Is there a class number associated with just "Animals"?
5. If I have a book of nature photography on an Animal "Special subject," do I choose TR729.A–Z as my call number?
6. If the book in front of you has the LCC number TR729.C69, what is the topic of the book?
7. What class number should you assign to a book of bark nature photography?

Browsing LCC in Classification Web

Now that you have a better sense of what LCC looks like in Classification Web, let's talk about how to navigate and browse it. This is the main menu of Classification Web (https://classificationweb.net):

Main Menu of Classification Web

From here, you can access the LCC schedules several different ways, which can be a bit confusing at first. You can click on either Browse LC Classification Schedules or Search LC Classification (the first two links on the main page of Classification Web). Or you can click on Outline (nestled between Usage and Subsets at the bottom of the screen) to see an outline of LCC. So what should you click on first?

It basically boils down to these choices:

1. Do you want to search the schedules directly by entering a class number and then browse around from there? If yes, then choose Browse LC Classification Schedules.
2. Do you know the topic and want to find the class number associated with that topic? If yes, then choose Search LC Classification, or possibly Browse/Search LC Subject Headings—I will explain more about this choice in chapter 13.
3. Do you want to start with an outline of the entire schedule and "drill down" to the number you need? If yes, then choose Outline.

We'll discuss *searching* LCC in a moment, but for now, let's discuss *browsing* LCC (the first link you see listed in Classification Web—Browse LC Classification Schedules). Selecting Browse LC Classification Schedules in Classification Web will lead you to a screen that is blank except for the following (once you have logged in, of course):

LCC Navigation Bar

This is the navigation bar. From here, you can browse or search for an LC class number or Cutter table, return to the menu, or navigate up and down the schedule using the arrow buttons. Also notice "(Enhanced Browser)" next to the search box. This is a reference to one of three different types of displays of LCC within Classification Web. You can choose the display type from the main menu of Classification Web (see the three options highlighted below):

Main Menu of Classification Web—Browser Types Highlighted

The *Enhanced Browser* is the default display type; it merges information from tables directly into the LCC schedules (we will talk more about tables in a later chapter). The *Standard Browser* provides links to tables and other class numbers rather than integrating the information into the schedules. The *Hierarchy Browser* provides the same integration as the Enhanced Browser, but instead of showing you all the information at once, it hyperlinks the entries that contain further hierarchy. Which browser type you choose comes down to preference more than anything else, though having table information incorporated into the schedules using the Enhanced or Hierarchy Browsers does come in very handy! For the sake of consistency, I will use only the Enhanced Browser in my screenshots throughout this book. Here are screenshots of PS3505.A87 (works by and about American author Willa Cather) viewed within each type of browser.

STANDARD BROWSER

Standard Browser

The reason why one class number and caption are highlighted is because that is the class number I typed into Browse to get to this screen. It does not have any further significance. In the Standard Browser, notice how the table needed to build the call number is hyperlinked. You must click on that link to view Table P–PZ40:

Table for authors (1 Cutter no.)

	Table for authors (1 Cutter no.)
	Collected works
	Including collected works in specific genres
P-PZ40 .x date	By date
(P-PZ40 .xA11-.xA13)	By editor
	Subarrangement by editor has been discontinued by the Library of Congress. Beginning in 2005, all collected works are subarranged by date
(P-PZ40 .xA14-.xA19)	Collected prose, poetry, plays, etc.
	For collected genres see P-PZ40 .x date
	Translations (Collected or selected)
P-PZ40 .xA199	Modern versions of early authors in the same language. By date
P-PZ40 .xA1995	Polyglot. By date
P-PZ40 .xA2	English. By date
P-PZ40 .xA3	French. By date
P-PZ40 .xA4	German. By date
P-PZ40 .xA5-.xA59	Other. By language (alphabetically) and date
P-PZ40 .xA6	Selected works. Selections. By date
P-PZ40 .xA61-.xZ458	Separate works. By title
	Biography and criticism
P-PZ40 .xZ4581-.xZ4589	Periodicals. Societies. Serials
P-PZ40 .xZ459	Dictionaries, indexes, etc. By date
P-PZ40 .xZ46	Autobiography, journals, memoirs. By date
P-PZ40 .xZ48	Letters (Collections). By date
	Including collections of letters to and from particular individuals
P-PZ40 .xZ5-.xZ999	General works

Table P–PZ40

ENHANCED BROWSER

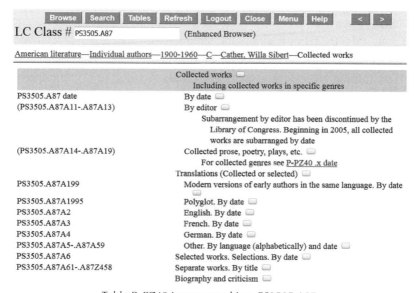

| Browse | Search | Tables | Refresh | Logout | Close | Menu | Help | < | > |

LC Class # PS3505.A87   (Enhanced Browser)

American literature—Individual authors—1900-1960—C—Cather, Willa Sibert

PS3505.A763	Carr, John Dickson, 1906-1977 Table P-PZ40
PS3505.A79327	Carter, Nick Table P-PZ40
	Pseudonym shared by multiple authors
	Carter, Ralph see PS3527.E598
PS3505.A85486	Castle, William R. (William Richard), 1878-1963 Table P-PZ40
PS3505.A87	Cather, Willa Sibert Table P-PZ40
PS3505.A896	Cauldwell, Samuel Milbank, 1862-1916 Table P-PZ40
	Cauliflower, Sebastian, 1893-1970 see PS3537.E362
PS3505.A97	Cayton, Susie Revels, 1870-1943 Table P-PZ40
	Challis, George, 1892-1944 see PS3511.A87
PS3505.H335	Chapin, Anna Alice, 1880-1920 Table P-PZ40
PS3505.H528	Chase, Virginia, 1902- Table P-PZ40
PS3505.H633	Chaze, Elliott Table P-PZ40
	Chaze, Lewis Elliott see PS3505.H633
PS3505.H684	Chester, George Randolph, 1869-1924 Table P-PZ40
PS3505.H716	Chetwood, John, 1859 Table P-PZ40
	Chin-lo-k'o, Chieh-k'o see PS3521.E735

Enhanced Browser

In the Enhanced Browser, Willa Cather's name is hyperlinked, not Table P–PZ40. Click on Cather's name, and Classification Web will automatically incorporate the table information into where you are in the schedules rather than requiring you to do so yourself. Here is a screenshot of Table P–PZ40 incorporated into Cather's class number:

| Browse | Search | Tables | Refresh | Logout | Close | Menu | Help | < | > |

LC Class # PS3505.A87   (Enhanced Browser)

American literature—Individual authors—1900-1960—C—Cather, Willa Sibert—Collected works

	Collected works
	Including collected works in specific genres
PS3505.A87 date	By date
(PS3505.A87A11-.A87A13)	By editor
	Subarrangement by editor has been discontinued by the Library of Congress. Beginning in 2005, all collected works are subarranged by date
(PS3505.A87A14-.A87A19)	Collected prose, poetry, plays, etc.
	For collected genres see P-PZ40 .x date
	Translations (Collected or selected)
PS3505.A87A199	Modern versions of early authors in the same language. By date
PS3505.A87A1995	Polyglot. By date
PS3505.A87A2	English. By date
PS3505.A87A3	French. By date
PS3505.A87A4	German. By date
PS3505.A87A5-.A87A59	Other. By language (alphabetically) and date
PS3505.A87A6	Selected works. Selections. By date
PS3505.A87A61-.A87Z458	Separate works. By title
	Biography and criticism

Table P–PZ40 Incorporated into PS3505.A87

HIERARCHY BROWSER

Browse	Search	Tables	Refresh	Logout	Close	Menu	Help	`<`	`>`

LC Class # PS3505.A87   (Hierarchy Browser)

American literature—Individual authors—1900-1960—C—Cather, Willa Sibert

PS3505.A763	Carr, John Dickson, 1906-1977 Table P-PZ40 ▢
PS3505.A79327	Carter, Nick Table P-PZ40 ▢
	Pseudonym shared by multiple authors
	Carter, Ralph see PS3527.E598 ▢
PS3505.A85486	Castle, William R. (William Richard), 1878-1963 Table P-PZ40 ▢
PS3505.A87	Cather, Willa Sibert Table P-PZ40 ▢
PS3505.A896	Cauldwell, Sanuel Milbank, 1862-1916 Table P-PZ40 ▢
	Cauliflower, Sebastian, 1893-1970 see PS3537.E362 ▢
PS3505.A97	Cayton, Susie Revels, 1870-1943 Table P-PZ40 ▢
	Challis, George, 1892-1944 see PS3511.A87 ▢
PS3505.H335	Chapin, Anna Alice, 1880-1920 Table P-PZ40 ▢
PS3505.H528	Chase, Virginia, 1902- Table P-PZ40 ▢
PS3505.H633	Chaze, Elliott Table P-PZ40 ▢
	Chaze, Lewis Elliott see PS3505.H633 ▢
PS3505.H684	Chester, George Randolph, 1869-1924 Table P-PZ40 ▢
PS3505.H716	Chetwood, John, 1859 Table P-PZ40 ▢
	Chin-lo-k'o, Chieh-k'o see PS3521.E735 ▢

Hierarchy Browser

PS3505.A87 in the Hierarchy Browser looks the same as it does in the Enhanced Browser. To see the difference, you have to click on Cather's hyperlinked name:

Browse	Search	Tables	Refresh	Logout	Close	Menu	Help	`<`	`>`

LC Class # PS3505.A87   (Hierarchy Browser)

American literature—Individual authors—1900-1960—C—Cather, Willa Sibert—Collected works

PS3505.A87 date-.A87A13	Collected works ▢
	Including collected works in specific genres
PS3505.A87A199-.A87A59	Translations (Collected or selected) ▢
PS3505.A87A6	Selected works. Selections. By date ▢
PS3505.A87A61-.A87Z458	Separate works. By title ▢
PS3505.A87Z4581-.A87Z999	Biography and criticism ▢
PS3505.A896	Cauldwell, Sanuel Milbank, 1862-1916 Table P-PZ40 ▢
PS3505.A896 date-.A896A13	Collected works ▢
	Including collected works in specific genres
PS3505.A896A199-.A896A59	Translations (Collected or selected) ▢
PS3505.A896A6	Selected works. Selections. By date ▢
PS3505.A896A61-.A896Z458	Separate works. By title ▢
PS3505.A896Z4581-.A896Z999	Biography and criticism ▢

Table P–PZ40 Incorporated into PS3505.A87

Notice how the main categories (Collected Works, Translations, and Biography and Criticism) are hyperlinked. You have to click on the hyperlink to see the subcategories (for example, By editor and By date under Collected Works).

Now that we have covered the different types of browsers, let's get back to the act of browsing itself. To illustrate, let's search the schedule for TX715 (American cookbooks post-1800) and click Browse or hit Enter on your keyboard (don't click on Search as that will bring up a different screen):

Browse	Search	Tables	Refresh	Logout	Close	Menu	Help		<	>

LC Class # TX715   (Enhanced Browser)

Home economics—Cooking—Cookbooks—1800-—American—General works

	American
	For French, German, etc., cookbooks published in America, see TX719, TX721, etc.
TX715	General works
TX715.2.A-Z	By style of cooking, A-Z
TX715.2.A47	African American cooking
TX715.2.C34	California style
	Hawaiian style see TX724.5.H3
TX715.2.L68	Louisiana style
TX715.2.M53	Midwestern style
TX715.2.N48	New England style
TX715.2.P32	Pacific Northwest style
	Pennsylvania Dutch style see TX721
TX715.2.S68	Southern style
TX715.2.S69	Southwestern style
TX715.2.W47	Western style
TX715.6	Canadian
TX715.8	Greenlandic
	Latin American
TX716.A1	General works

TX715—American Cookbooks Post-1800

First, look at the "breadcrumbs" toward the top of the screen, under LC Class #. These tell you where you are in the schedule's hierarchy:

Home economics—Cooking—Cookbooks—1800-—American—General works

TX715 Breadcrumbs

The breadcrumbs are selectable if you are using the Enhanced or Hierarchy Browser. For example, if you click on "Cooking," it will take you back to that part of the schedule in the hierarchy.

Click on the back button (<) at the top of the screen to move back one page, and click on the forward button (>) to move forward one page:

Navigation Bar Arrows

QUICK TIP . . .

Breadcrumbs can be very handy when you find yourself "lost" in the schedules after too many clicks on the back and forward buttons! Also, use them to double-check a selected class number. Search for the class number (plus Cutter, if applicable) or double-click on it within the schedules and check the breadcrumbs that appear to ensure that you chose the correct one.

Remember how I said before that there was another way to reach the LCC schedules, by drilling down from an outline? In order to do that, go back to the main menu and select Outline from the lower section:

Log Out - Preferences - Usage - Outline - Subsets - Bookmarks - Help
Auto Login Menu - Diagnostics - Legal Notices - Contacts - User Group - Home

Link on Main Menu to LCC Outline

This will bring you to the following page:

Classification Outline

A -- GENERAL WORKS
B -- PHILOSOPHY. PSYCHOLOGY. RELIGION
C -- AUXILIARY SCIENCES OF HISTORY
D -- HISTORY: GENERAL AND OLD WORLD
E -- HISTORY: AMERICA
F -- HISTORY: AMERICA
G -- GEOGRAPHY. ANTHROPOLOGY. RECREATION
H -- SOCIAL SCIENCES
J -- POLITICAL SCIENCE
K -- LAW
L -- EDUCATION
M -- MUSIC AND BOOKS ON MUSIC
N -- FINE ARTS
P -- LANGUAGE AND LITERATURE
Q -- SCIENCE
R -- MEDICINE
S -- AGRICULTURE
T -- TECHNOLOGY
U -- MILITARY SCIENCE
V -- NAVAL SCIENCE
Z -- BIBLIOGRAPHY. LIBRARY SCIENCE.
INFORMATION RESOURCES (GENERAL)

LCC Outline

From here you can browse around in the schedules by clicking on the class number you want to explore and continue clicking on more specific topics until you research the desired class number. For example, if you select "T—Technology," you find yourself in the browser here:

| Browse | Search | Tables | Refresh | Logout | Close | Menu | Help | < | > |

LC Class # T   (Hierarchy Browser)

Technology (General)

T1-995	Technology (General) ▢
TA1-2040	Engineering (General). Civil engineering (General) ▢
TC1-1800	Hydraulic engineering ▢
	For municipal water supply see TD201-500.2 ▢
	For hydraulic machinery see TJ840.A2-.A3 ▢
TC1501-1800	Ocean engineering ▢
	Cf. GC1000-1023 Marine resources ▢
	Cf. TN291.5 Ocean mining ▢
TD1-1066	Environmental technology. Sanitary engineering ▢
	Including the promotion and conservation of the public health, comfort, and convenience by the control of the environment
	Cf. GE170-190 Environmental policy ▢
	Cf. GF51 Human beings and the environment ▢
	Cf. RA565-600 Environmental health ▢
	Cf. TH6014-6085 Environmental engineering in buildings ▢
TE1-450	Highway engineering. Roads and pavements ▢
	Cf. HD9717.5.R6-.R64 Road construction industry ▢
	Cf. HE331-380 Traffic engineering; economics of roads ▢
	Cf. QH545.R62 Environmental effects ▢
	Cf. TD888.R62 Air pollution ▢

T—Technology Class

Click on the hyperlinked caption to go to those parts of the LCC schedules. For example, if the resource you are cataloging is about ocean engineering, click on the hyperlinked "Ocean engineering," which is covered in LC class numbers TC1501–1800. This is a range of class numbers; assume that the letters at the beginning of the range apply to the numbers after the hyphen. Therefore, TC1501–1800 literally means TC1501 through TC1800.

There are multiple ways to enter and view the LCC schedules. Browsing can be beneficial when you know the general topic of a work but are not certain how to narrow the focus. When browsing the schedules, pay close attention to the breadcrumbs at the top of the screen, as well as the instructions surrounding the captions. "See" and "Cf." notes can be very useful when you are presented with various options.

EXERCISES

1. From the main menu of Classification Web, click on Browse LC Classification Schedules and type "BJ66" in the text box next to LC Class #. What is the caption associated with that class number?
2. Examine the breadcrumbs for the topic in question #1—what is the topic at the beginning of the breadcrumbs? What is a work assigned BJ66 about?
3. Go to the LCC Outline from the main menu of Classification Web and click on "L—Education." What is the class number range for "Theory and practice of education"?
4. Does the "Theory and practice of education" include the topic of someone's right to education?

8

Searching LCC in Classification Web

Now that you know how to browse and move around in the LCC schedules in Classification Web, let's talk about how to search. Once again, there are multiple ways you can do this. First, you can select LC Classification Search from the main menu. Or, from the navigation bar, you can click on the Search tab at the top to bring up the search screen:

	Search	Reset	Logout	Close	Menu	Help

LC Classification Search

Caption ❶
Keyword ❶
Index term ❶
Caption or index term ❶
Classification number ❶

Search tips and options

LC Classification Search

Here is what the above terminology means:

Caption: The most specific descriptor for a class number. So "General works" for TX715.

Keyword: Searches most of the indexes.

Index term: Searches see references (variant forms). For example, searching "boot industry" brings up the appropriate class "Footwear. Shoes."

Caption or index term: Searches both captions and index terms (variants).

Classification number: Searches the class number, as well as any "see" references. Browsing this is like using the Standard Browser.

QUICK TIP . . .

If you are having difficulty finding what you are looking for using one way of searching, try other types. For example, if performing a caption search is not yielding fruitful results, try using the index term search.

Using an example will help you better understand how each type of search works. Let's pretend we are cataloging the following work:

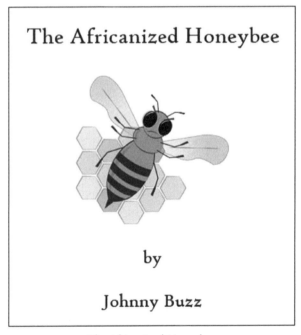

The Africanized Honeybee

If you type "Africanized honeybee" in the caption search box and click on Search or hit Enter, your results should look like this:

LC Classification Search: Caption

Africanized honeybee (2)

SF538.5.A37	Africanized honeybee ▭
[SF539.5-.6]	Africanized honeybee ▭

Africans (31)

DU122.A35	Africans ▭
DS339.3.A34	Africans ▭
DG659.6.A37	Africans ▭
DB851.57.A37	Africans ▭
D1056.2.A38	Africans ▭
DB34.A47	Africans ▭
E184.A24	Africans ▭
HV640.5.A3	Africans ▭
PR830.A39	Africans ▭

Africanized Honeybee Caption Search

There are two results for Africanized honeybee, SF538.5.A37 and [SF539.5–.6], both of which have the caption "Africanized honey-bee." In order to determine the difference between the results, click on SF538.5.A37, [SF539.5–.6], or both. The reason why the second entry is enclosed in square brackets is because there is a range of classification numbers representing this particular entry: SF539.5 through SF539.6. It is not a very long range but a range nonetheless!

If you click on SF538.5.A37, the next screen should look like this:

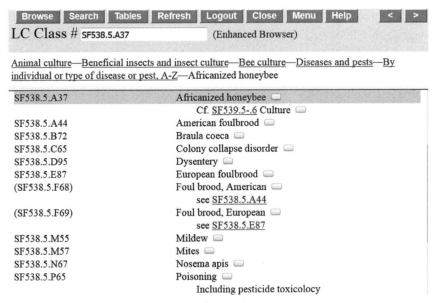

Africanized Honeybee Pest

At this point, it is helpful to remember what we discussed in the last chapter—namely, the discussion about the highlighted entry and the "breadcrumbs" toward the top of the screen. The highlighted entry is the class number and Cutter we selected on the previous page (SF538.5.A37). By examining the breadcrumbs closely, we can see that, in this context, the Africanized honeybee is treated as a type of "disease or pest" within bee culture. Let's assume the book we are cataloging is not about the Africanized honeybee as a type of "disease or pest," so let's go back to the previous page and look at the other entry: [SF539.5–.6].

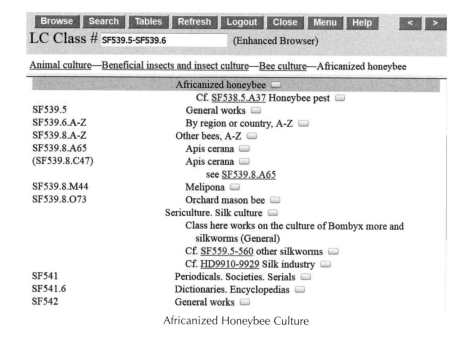

Africanized Honeybee Culture

Looking at the breadcrumbs on this screen, we can see that SF539.5 and SF539.6 should be applied to works about Africanized honeybee culture.

I will return to this page in the next chapter about building basic LCC call numbers, but before I do that, I want to investigate the other ways we can search LCC. To refresh your memory, here are our options:

LC Classification Search

We have already explored searching "Africanized honeybee" as a caption, so let's search for it using the keyword search. When we do, here are the results:

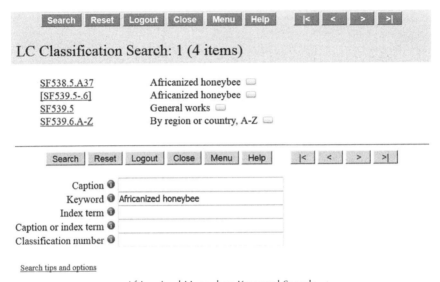

Africanized Honeybee Keyword Search

As mentioned previously, the keyword search results show us everywhere "Africanized honeybee" is found in LCC—the two results we explored above, as well as the SF539.5–.6 span broken down: SF539.5 for general works on Africanized honeybees and SF539.6.A–Z for Africanized honeybees by region or country (I will explain what this means in the next chapter).

Keyword searching is helpful if you are uncertain about which caption you are looking for or when you simply want to see what LCC has on a given topic. For example, here are most of my results when I perform a keyword search for "chocolate":

NK4696.37	Chocolate collectibles ▭
HD8039.C5-.C52	Chocolate industry employees ▭
HD9200	Cocoa. Chocolate ▭
F868.I2	Imperial County ▭
TX767.C5	Chocolate ▭
TX767.W48	White chocolate ▭
Z5776.C5	Chocolate. Cocoa ▭
TX817.C4	Chocolate ▭
[TP638-655]	Chocolate, coffee, tea, etc. ▭
TP640	Cacao. Chocolate. Cocoa ▭
TP645	Coffee ▭
TP650	Tea ▭
TP655.A-Z	Others, A-Z ▭
[RM240-251]	Tea. Coffee. Chocolate. Cocoa ▭
RM240	General works ▭
RM241	Chocolate. Cocoa ▭
RM246	Coffee ▭
RM251	Tea ▭
RM666.C524	Chocolate ▭
PN6231.C33	Chocolate ▭
TP638	General works ▭
GT2920.C3	Chocolate ▭
QP144.C46	Chocolate. Cocoa ▭

Chocolate Keyword Search

An index term search checks cross-references (i.e., variant terms) associated with the topic. The Help section of Classification Web mentions that this search pulls from MARC field 753 in the authority record for the classification number (the field for an "uncontrolled index term"). Don't worry too much about the authority record; the important point to remember is that index terms are not the official terms associated with a classification number, but they can help guide you to what *is* the official term: the caption. When I perform an index search for "Africanized honeybee," this is the result—the same entries we encountered previously, but the specific topics are stated more explicitly:

LC Classification Search: Index term

Africanized honeybee: Bee culture
    [SF539.5-.6]   Africanized honeybee ▢

Africanized honeybee: Bee diseases and pests
    SF538.5.A37   Africanized honeybee ▢

Africans: Christianity
    BR737.A37   Africans ▢

Africans: Discovery of America
    E109.A35   African ▢

Africanized Honeybee Index Search

The index search can be very helpful when a caption search produces results too general or specific. Going back to our Chocolate example, you can see how many times the caption "Chocolate" appears—yikes! However, an index search for "Chocolate" yields hyperlinked results containing more information and context for each classification number. Notice above the class numbers it says, for example, "Chocolate: Bibliography: Home economics" and "Chocolate: Nonalcoholic beverages":

LC Classification Search: Index term

Chocolate: Bibliography: Home economics
    Z5776.C5   Chocolate. Cocoa ▢

Chocolate: Nonalcoholic beverages
    [TP638-655]   Chocolate, coffee, tea, etc. ▢

Chocolate: Nutrition
    QP144.C46   Chocolate. Cocoa ▢

Chocolate: Recipes
    TX767.C5   Chocolate ▢

Chocolate: Therapeutics
    RM666.C524   Chocolate ▢

Chocolate beverages: Cooking
    TX817.C4   Chocolate ▢

Chocolate Index Search

Caption and index searching combines the results of the separate caption and index searches described above, so I won't go into further explanation here except to show you what happens when I perform a caption and index search for "Africanized honeybee":

LC Classification Search: Caption or Index term

Africanized honeybee
    SF538.5.A37   Africanized honeybee ⊖
    [SF539.5-.6]   Africanized honeybee ⊖

Africanized honeybee: Bee culture
    [SF539.5-.6]   Africanized honeybee ⊖

Africanized honeybee: Bee diseases and pests
    SF538.5.A37   Africanized honeybee ⊖

Africanized Honeybee Caption and Index Search

   The final type of search you can perform in Classification Web is the classification number search. If I search for SF539.5 (General works on Africanized honeybees), then I receive these results containing the classification number I searched for, as well as the classification numbers surrounding it:

LC Classification Search: Classification number

SF539.5-.6
    [SF539.5-.6]   Africanized honeybee ⊖
    SF538.5.A37   Africanized honeybee ⊖

SF539.5
    SF539.5   General works ⊖

SF539.6.A-Z
    SF539.6.A-Z   By region or country, A-Z ⊖

SF539.8.A-Z
    SF539.8.A-Z   Other bees, A-Z ⊖

SF539.8.A65
    SF539.8.A65   Apis cerana ⊖

Africanized Honeybee Classification Search

I would like to emphasize here that there is no one "right" way to search in Classification Web. The type of search you choose depends upon what information you already have and what you hope to learn. In fact, I recommend trying different types of searches if one way doesn't yield the results you hoped to find.

EXERCISES

1. Perform a caption search and then an index search for "Cattle." Find the classification number associated with cattle as air cargo.
2. ZA4080 is associated with what topic?
3. Search for "Apples" using the caption and index search. Which classification number is associated with the food processing of apples?
4. Use various search techniques to find the appropriate class number for higher education, specifically focusing on higher education in developing countries.
5. Perform a keyword search for "Phones." What type of phones are in the captions of the search results?

9

Basic LCC Call Number Building

In order to build an LCC call number, we must move beyond browsing and searching for class numbers. For example, it's good to know that SF539.5 is the class number for general works on Africanized honeybees, but where do you go from there? In many cases, adding a main entry Cutter and the publication date will suffice, but not always. That is why it is important to understand how to read the LCC schedules to know whether or not you need to do something else.

Let's continue with our previous example, *The Africanized Honeybee* by Johnny Buzz, but add the fact that it was published in 1989.

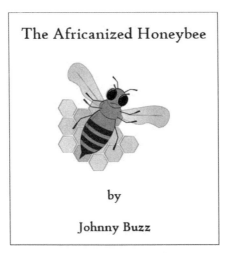

The Africanized Honeybee

If you recall from the last chapter, I mentioned that this book is about Africanized honeybees generally and not focused on them as pests, so we should focus our attention on this range of class numbers: SF539.5 through SF539.6 (if you don't remember why, I recommend reviewing the last chapter). Here they are in Classification Web, enclosed in a rectangle:

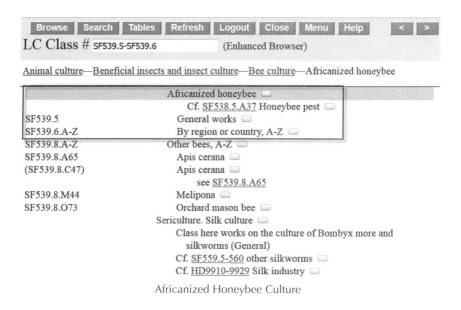

Africanized Honeybee Culture

We have two choices: SF539.5 for general works on Africanized honeybees and SF539.6.A–Z for Africanized honeybees by region or country. Since the book we are cataloging doesn't appear to be about Africanized honeybees of a certain locale, it's safe to say that we can rule out SF539.6.A–Z (By region or country) and choose SF539.5 (General works). The "General works" caption is one of the most common captions you will see in LCC. Unless the work you are cataloging is about a more specific topic or the topic in a specific place or time period, the "General works" class number is usually the way to go.

As we discussed in a previous chapter on Cutters, sometimes there will be a Cutter after the class number representing an additional topic or place, as in SF539.8.M44 (SF539.8 representing "Other bees" and .M44 representing the Melipona bee in particular). However, there is no Cutter after SF539.5, and there are no instructions on what else to add. Therefore, you should proceed to add a main entry Cutter after the class number: SF539.5 + main entry Cutter. This is the case for all class numbers that don't specify a Cutter or Cutters after the class number, either in the schedules themselves or within a table. So what is our main entry Cutter? As I discussed in earlier chapters, the main entry Cutter will either be the main author of the work (if there are multiple authors, then usually the first person listed on the title page) or the title if there is no main author.

QUICK TIP . . .

Unless LCC specifies that an additional Cutter is needed after a class number, the main entry Cutter will be the first (and only) Cutter after the class number.

Johnny Buzz is the main author of *The Africanized Honeybee*, so we need to Cutter the first three letters of this last name. Buzz begins with a consonant ("B"), so start Cuttering on line 4:

1. After initial vowels								
for the second letter:	b	d	l-m	n	p	r	s-t	u-y
use the number-------→	2	3	4	5	6	7	8	9
2. After the initial letter S								
for the second letter:	a	ch	e	h-i	m-p	t	u	w-z
use the number-------→	2	3	4	5	6	7	8	9
3. After the initial letters Qu								
for the second letter:	a	e	i	o	r	t	y	
use the numbers-----→	3	4	5	6	7	8	9	
For the initial letters **Qa-QT** Use: **2-29**								
4. After other Initial consonants								
for the second letter:	a	e	i	o	r	u	y	
use the number ------→	3	4	5	6	7	8	9	
5. For expansion to an additional number								
for the next letter:	a-d	e-h	i-l	m-o	p-s	t-v	w-z	
use the number-------→	3	4	5	6	7	8	9	

LCC Cutter Table—Buzz

Buzz = .B89

We know that the book was published in 1989 because I told you that at the very beginning of this chapter, so let's put it all together:

SF539.5 = general works on Africanized honeybees
.B89 = Cutter for the main entry (Buzz)
1989 = publication year

SF539.5 .B89 1989
In MARC, we would write this as:
050 _4 $a SF539.5 $b .B89 1989

Use the 050 MARC field for most Library of Congress Classification call numbers. You could also use the 090 field, but it is for locally as-signed LC-type call numbers. The first indicator of the 050 field tells us if the work is in the Library of Congress's collection (0 = yes and 1 = no; or you can just leave this blank if you don't know or, in our case, you are cataloging a fake item!). The second indicator tells us whether or not the Library of Congress created the call number (0 = yes and 4 = no; or, once again, you can simply leave this indicator blank).

QUICK TIP . . .

For those of you using MARC: Not all institutions will use MARC field 050 for Library of Congress Classification call numbers. Sometimes they will use MARC field 090. I will use the 050 field in my examples and in the end-of-chapter exercise answers, but you are welcome to convert 050 _4 to 090 _ _ (the underscores represent blank spaces).

Let's again pretend that Johnny Buzz was a prolific writer on Africanized honeybees and that he wrote another book about Africanized honeybees, this time focusing on the bee within the United States (published in 1992).

The Africanized Honeybee in the United States

We know from Classification Web that we can add further information about the region or country at SF539.6. But it says specifically SF539.6.A–Z. What does the .A–Z mean? Does that mean we add .A–Z after SF539.6 to show that our work is about Africanized honeybees in the United States? No, it doesn't! The .A–Z is a placeholder for the first Cutter of the call number, in this case representing the specific region or country referred to in the work. The Cutter for the region or country should be between A and Z. This use of A–Z is very common throughout the LCC schedules. For example, here is another entry where we can specify mobile home living by US region or state (TX1107.2.A–Z) or by other regions or countries (TX1107.4.A–Z):

	Mobile home living ⬚
	Cf. GV198.5-.7 Mobile home living ⬚
TX1100	Periodicals, societies, etc. ⬚
TX1105	General works ⬚
TX1106	Juvenile works ⬚
	By region or country ⬚
	United States ⬚
TX1107	General works ⬚
TX1107.2.A-Z	By region or state, A-Z ⬚
TX1107.4.A-Z	Other regions or countries, A-Z ⬚

Mobile Home Living

Other A–Z entries have nothing to do with geographic places but allow you to provide further detail about the topic. For example, if your work is about a special form or flavor of ice cream, use TX796, and the first Cutter should represent the special form or flavor:

	Ice creams and ices ⬚
TX795.A1	Periodicals, societies, etc. ⬚
TX795.A2-Z	General works ⬚
TX796.A-Z	Special forms, flavors, etc. A-Z ⬚
TX796.I45	Ice cream sandwiches ⬚

Ice Creams and Ices

LCC provides TX796.I45 (Ice cream sandwiches) as an example, but you can create a Cutter for another ice cream or ice form, such as TX796 .P67 for a work on popsicles (use the LCC Cutter table to Cutter "Popsicles"). The Cutter .P67 falls between A and Z, so it is acceptable.

However, you shouldn't use the LCC Cutter table for regions or countries. Region and country Cutters are predetermined, and you can find them in the free *Classification and Shelflisting Manual* at G300 (https://www.loc.gov/aba/publications/FreeCSM/G300.pdf) or in the back matter of this book. Countries and regions are listed alphabetically. You can use the Cataloging Calculator (http://calculate.alptown.com), a free web-based program that supplies the Cutter for whatever region or country you type in (choose the Geog. Cutter radio button before you type the place name). US states and Canadian provinces also have predetermined Cutters. You can find them in the *Classification and Shelflisting Manual* at G302 (https://www.loc.gov/aba/publications/FreeCSM/G302.pdf), in the back matter of this book, or through the Cataloging Calculator.

In both sources mentioned above, the Cutter for the United States is U6. If the class number for Africanized honeybees by region or country is SF539.6 and the first Cutter should be United States, then our call number should look like this so far:

SF539.6 .U6
SF539.6 = Africanized honeybees by region or country
.U6 = United States (always put a period in front of the first Cutter)

This is a great start, but we are not done yet. What if we have multiple books in our collection on Africanized honeybees in the United States? We need to make sure that each resource has a unique call number. We can achieve this by adding a second Cutter to our call number: one for the main entry, Johnny Buzz. This way, all books on this topic will be placed together on the shelf and then organized within the topic primarily by the main author of the work. We know from our earlier call number building that Buzz should be Cuttered B89, so add that, as well as the publication year, to the class number and first Cutter:

SF539.6 .U6 B89 1992
SF539.6 = Africanized honeybees by region or country
.U6 = United States (always put a period in front of the first Cutter)
B89 = the main entry (Buzz)—no period is needed in front of the second Cutter
1992 = publication year

And in MARC:

050 _4 $a SF539.6.U6 $b B89 1992

In MARC, always put the subfield $b in front of the last Cutter. If there is only one Cutter, put it in front of that Cutter. If there are two Cutters (as above), put it in front of the second Cutter.

It is important to pay close attention to the Cutter(s) following a class number since they "reserve" a Cutter or a range of Cutters you can use to represent a topic, time period, or format. Let's look at a previous example to illustrate the need to heed those Cutters!

	Ice creams and ices
TX795.A1	Periodicals, societies, etc.
TX795.A2-Z	General works
TX796.A-Z	Special forms, flavors, etc. A-Z
TX796.I45	Ice cream sandwiches

Ice Creams and Ices

Earlier we discussed that TX796 allows us to Cutter by "Special forms, flavors, etc." of ice cream and ices. If you look at TX795, you will see that TX795.A1 is reserved for "Periodicals, societies, etc." about ice creams and ices (for example, *Ice Cream Monthly*). General works about ice creams and ices should also be classed in TX795, but the first Cutter should be between .A2 and .Z. This entry is *not* saying that your first Cutter should be .A2 or .A2–Z, nor is it specifying a Cutter you should use for general works on this topic. It is saying that your main entry Cutter should be between .A2 and .Z. For example, if we are cataloging the book *Ice Cream Is Yummy!* by Rock E. Road, published in 2010 (a general work on ice cream), the call number should be TX795.R63 2010. The Cutter for the author, Road, is .R63, which falls safely between .A2 and .Z. Pretty much any author or title Cutter will fit between .A2 and .Z, but there may be class numbers with much more limited Cutter ranges where you will need to adjust a main entry Cutter to fit within it. This example is a great illustration of how Cutters can mean so many different things depending on the situation.

One final note before we move into advanced call number building. On occasion, you will see class numbers surrounded by parentheses, as in the screenshot below:

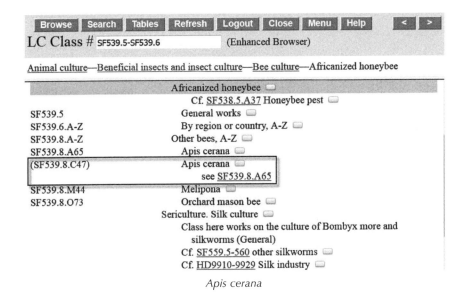

Apis cerana

Parentheses around a class number mean that it is no longer valid. Use the class number after "see" instead. In the above example, if you have a work on *Apis cerana*, use SF539.8.A65 and *not* SF539.8.C47.

Call number building becomes easier the more you do it. Many of the same patterns and instructions appear again and again in LCC, so what seems incomprehensible at first (like the many A–Zs!) will be second nature before you know it. In the next chapter, we will dig deeper into the LCC schedules to decipher some slightly more complex instructions.

EXERCISE

Construct LCC call numbers for the following works. Feel free to answer with or without MARC coding.

1. A work on paper-bag cooking by Desmond Quick, published in 1970.
2. A book of nature photography featuring roses by Roxanne Offerman, published in 1986.

3. A work on the veterinary anatomy of camels by Tania Fernandez, published in 2012.

4. A work on agricultural structures in New Zealand by Pat Alonso, published in 1983.

5. A work on computer crimes in California by Dorothy Pfeiffer, published in 2001.

6. A *directory* of landscape architecture in Ohio by Milo Sandyman, published in 1999.

7. A *periodical* on mathematical logic by Declan McSweeny, published in 2016.

8. A general work on the history of dollhouses by Max Schaefer, published in 1990.

9. A work on the history of dollhouses in Japan by Hina Ooki, published in 2015.

10. A book titled (and about) *An Introduction to Glass Blowing*, edited by Julia Glasbläser (this is a title main entry), probably published in 1968.

10

Advanced Call Number Building Using Tables (Including the Translation and Biography Tables)

In this chapter, I will discuss more complex call number building, primarily through the use of tables—lists of notations that you can use to further build a call number. They can either be embedded in the schedules and apply to specific class numbers (we will talk more about these in the next chapter) or they can be outside of the schedules and applied across class numbers (or, at the least, within a specific range of class numbers). In this chapter, I will focus on the latter type, including the Translation and Biography Tables.

Unlike classification schemes such as Dewey Decimal, most LCC tables are not applicable to all areas of LCC. For example, Table P–PZ40 can be applied only to class numbers in the P (Language and Literature) class, not to all classes. When you are in the LCC schedules, you can access tables directly through the Tables button at the top of screen and by typing in a table number:

Navigation Bar Tables

However, if you are using the Enhanced or Hierarchy Browser, tables will be embedded or hyperlinked in the schedules, so there is rarely a need to search for them directly. In the LCC PDFs, the tables are included in the "text" documents, sandwiched between the schedules and the index.

In most cases, entries in the LCC schedules will tell you when a specific table should be applied, as in this example at HD3861 where Table H73 can be applied if you want more specificity:

HD3861.A-Z   By region or country, A-Z
                                         Subarrange each country by Table <u>H73</u>
                    HD3861 Table

Let's go through an example to see how LCC tables are used. You are cataloging this book about dog shows, specifically in the US state of California, published in 1999:

Dog Shows in California

Here is the area of LCC applicable to the work in hand:

	Dog shows and competitive events
	Including conformation or bench shows
SF425	General works
SF425.13	Juvenile works
	Including Junior Showmanship
SF425.14.A-Z	International. By place, A-Z
	National, state and local. By region or country
	United States
SF425.15	General works
SF425.16.A-Z	By region or state, A-Z
	Subarrange each state by Table S3a
SF425.18.A-Z	Other regions or countries, A-Z
	Subarrange each country by Table S3a
SF425.2	Judging. Standards
SF425.3	Show dogs

Dog Shows and Competitive Events

According to LCC, we can class works on dog shows and competitive events within a particular nation, state, or local place starting at SF425.15 (general works on dog shows within the United States). Since our work is about dog shows in California, SF425.16 is most relevant:

	Dog shows and competitive events
	Including conformation or bench shows
SF425	General works
SF425.13	Juvenile works
	Including Junior Showmanship
SF425.14.A-Z	International. By place, A-Z
	National, state and local. By region or country
	United States
SF425.15	General works
SF425.16.A-Z	By region or state, A-Z
	Subarrange each state by Table S3a
SF425.18.A-Z	Other regions or countries, A-Z
	Subarrange each country by Table S3a
SF425.2	Judging. Standards
SF425.3	Show dogs

SF425.16 By Region or State

As I have discussed previously, the A–Z after SF425.16 is determined by what it says in the caption. In this context, the A–Z represents the

Cutter range for the specific US region or state. According to the *Classification and Shelflisting Manual* G302 (https://www.loc.gov/aba/publications/FreeCSM/G302.pdf), California should be Cuttered .C2, so our call number should begin with SF425.16 .C2 (dogs shows in California). However, note the instruction underneath "By region or state, A–Z": "Subarrange each state by Table S3a."

If you click on the hyperlinked S3a, you will see this:

| Browse | Search | Schedules | Refresh | Logout | Close | Menu | Help | | < | > |

Table ID and LC Class # | _____ | (Enhanced Browser)

Subarrangement for Cutter-number countries, states, islands, etc.

	Subarrangement for Cutter-number countries, states, islands, etc. ▢
S3a .x	General works ▢
S3a .x2A-.x2Z	Local, A-Z ▢

Table S3a

This particular table allows for "Subarrangement for Cutter-number countries, states, islands, etc.," but what does all this mean? What is it saying to do? Let's break it down:

S3a on the left-hand side of the page is the name of the table, and we can ignore it for the purposes of constructing a call number. The use of the lowercase "x" is pretty common in LCC; it is a placeholder for the first Cutter, which in this case should be the Cutter for the individual US region or state (California in our example). For general works (which is what we have), nothing else needs to be done except to add the main entry Cutter and the publication date:

SF425.16 .C2 R84 1999
SF425.16 = dog shows by US region or state
.C2 = California
R84 = the main entry, Ruff
1999 = date of publication

However, there is another option in Table S3a:

S3a .x2A–.x2Z   Local, A–Z

"Local, A–Z" is a common caption in LCC, both in the schedules and in tables. In a nutshell, it means any geographic area hierarchically smaller than state level, like counties and cities. This does not apply to the above example, but let's assume you are asked to catalog another book on dog shows specifically in the city of Los Angeles, California, by Fido Quinoa, published in 2014. If we want to include Los Angeles in the call number, we can do that, but we have to be careful about how we do it. Which brings me to this:

.x2A–.x2Z

What does this mean? Remember that the lowercase "x" is a place-holder for the first Cutter, which can remain .C2 since the city of Los Angeles is in the US state of California. After the "x" there is a "2." This means that you need to place a "2" at the end of the first Cutter (.C22 = California [.C2] + "2" to indicate that the second Cutter will be a local place name). This "2" is very important because it signifies that the second Cutter will not represent the main entry but a local place name. The "A" and "Z" represent the second Cutter, which should be the "local" place name: Los Angeles for our work (I will use L6 to represent Los Angeles. It is common to Cutter out only one letter beyond the initial letter when you Cutter non–main entry names and titles). Therefore, the call number for our book on dog shows specifically in the city of Los Angeles, California, by Fido Quinoa, published in 2014, should look like this:

SF425.16 .C22 L6 2014
SF425.16 = dog shows by US region or state
.C22 = California (.C2) + "2" to indicate that the second Cutter *will not* be
the main entry, but a local place name
L6 = Los Angeles
2014 = publication year

Note how I did not include a Cutter for the main entry, the author Quinoa, in the above call number. If you recall from earlier chapters, you cannot have more than two Cutters per call number. My two Cutter "slots" are reserved according to the LCC instructions, so I cannot add a third Cutter for the author. If we don't include something about the author in the call number, then works on the same topic but published in a different year will look the same except for differing publication years. For example, a work on dog shows in Los Angeles, California, by Charlie G. Shepherd, published in 2015, would have this call number: SF425.16 .C22 L6 2015—very similar to the work by Fido Quinoa!

In the earlier chapter on dates, I mentioned that if the only difference between call numbers is the date, the call numbers represent different editions of the same work. Therefore, if we have two or more works on the same topic but written by different authors, we need to do something else to our call numbers to ensure unique call numbers.

This is not necessarily a big problem. If your institution holds only Fido Quinoa's work on dog shows in Los Angeles, California, and it is unlikely that you will receive further works on the topic, then the above call number may be sufficient. Moreover, if you don't need the added specificity of including Los Angeles in the call number (for example, you don't have a lot of dog show books and adding the local place Cutter is overkill), then you can choose to keep the call number at a broader level to ensure that the author Cutter is included:

SF425.16 .C2 Q56 2014
SF425.16 = dog shows by US region or state
.C2 = California (.C2)
Q56 = Quinoa, the main entry
2014 = publication year

This call number will allow you to keep all dog show works together by state and then organized by main entry.

But let's say for the sake of this lesson that your institution does collect a lot of resources on dog shows (for example, you work for a dog show historical society), and you need to organize by local place within a region or state, as well as the author's name. What do you do? The *Classification and Shelflisting Manual* instruction G055 has the solution for most situations (there may be a few where this won't work). Instead of adding another Cutter, add another digit to the second Cutter to represent the main entry. Use line 5 of the LCC Cutter table to create a number from the first letter of the main entry. The first letter of "Quinoa" is "q," which is represented by the number "7" on line 5 of the Cutter table:

1. After initial **vowels**

	b	d	l-m	n	p	r	s-t	u-y
for the second letter:								
use the number-------→	2	3	4	5	6	7	8	9

2. After the initial letter **S**

	a	ch	e	h-i	m-p	t	u	w-z
for the second letter:								
use the number-------→	2	3	4	5	6	7	8	9

3. After the initial letters **Qu**

	a	e	i	o	r	t	y
for the second letter:							
use the numbers-----→	3	4	5	6	7	8	9

For the initial letters **Qa-QT**
Use: **2-29**

4. After other **Initial consonants**

	a	e	i	o	r	u	y
for the second letter:							
use the number ------→	3	4	5	6	7	8	9

5. For **expansion** to an additional number

	a-d	e-h	i-l	m-o	p-s	t-v	w-z
for the next letter:							
use the number-------→	3	4	5	6	7	8	9

LCC Cutter Table—Expansion

Place it at the end of the second Cutter (L67).

Here is the updated call number for a book on dog shows specifically in the city of Los Angeles, California, by Fido Quinoa, published in 2014:

SF425.16 .C22 L67 2014
SF425.16 = dog shows by US region or state
.C22 = California (.C2) + "2" to indicate that the second Cutter *will not* be the main entry but a local place name
L67 = Los Angeles (L6) + "7" (representing "q," the first letter of "Quinoa") from line 5 of the Cutter table
2014 = publication year

By using this method, you will ensure that other works on this specific topic will stay in order on the shelf by main entry:

SF425.16 .C22 L63 2014 (a work by Davis)
SF425.16 .C22 L67 2014 (a work by Quinoa)
SF425.16 .C22 L68 2014 (a work by Thomas)

QUICK TIP . . .

If your two Cutter "slots" are taken, use line 5 on the Cutter table to Cutter the first letter of the main entry (for example, the first letter of the main author's last name). Place that number at the end of the second Cutter to ensure that the call number is unique and keeps works on the same topic alphabetized by main entry on the shelf.

Getting back to the use of tables, if you are using LCC within Classification Web, sometimes the contents of a table will be applied directly to an entry if you are using the Enhanced or Hierarchy Browser. To demonstrate what I mean, let's look at a few entries at HD9999:

HD9999.C25-.C254	Cans Table H21
HD9999.C26-.C264	Caps and closures Table H21
HD9999.C27-.C274	Car wash Table H21
	Carriages and wagons see HD9709.5
	Caskets see HD9999.C65-.C67
HD9999.C38-.C384	Charcoal Table H21

HD9999 Table H21

Notice how "Table H21" is right after most of the captions, but it is not hyperlinked. If you click on the hyperlinked "Car wash," for example, you will see this:

HD9999.C27	Periodicals. Societies. Serials
HD9999.C272	General works. History
	Including biography
HD9999.C273A-.C273Z	By region or country, A-Z
HD9999.C274A-.C274Z	Firms, A-Z

Car Wash with Table H21 Applied

If you look up Table H21 separately using the tables search, this is what you will see:

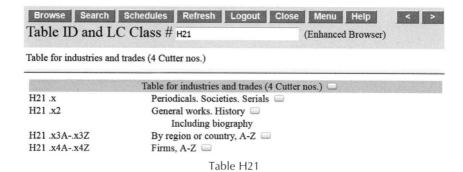
Table H21

Note how the contents of Table H21 are applied specifically to the entry for "Car wash" at HD9999.C27. By automatically applying the contents of a table to a specific entry in LCC, Classification Web reduces the number of steps you need to take when building a call number using a table. This way of utilizing tables is very common in the Language and Literature class P, which I will discuss more in depth in chapter 12.

If we return to the "Car wash" entry at HD9999.C27, you will see that many of the same concepts we discussed earlier in the chapter are applicable here as well. Let's say we are cataloging a work on the history of the car wash by Eleanor Lisbeth, published in 2011. You don't need to look at Table H21 directly. Just look again at the application of Table H21 at HD9999 .C27 and you can see that history works are assigned the class number and Cutter HD9999.C272. No other Cutters are assigned within the schedule, so we add the main entry Cutter (Lisbeth = L57) and the publication year:

HD9999.C272 L57 2011

If the work was about car washes in Mexico by Eleanor Lisbeth, published in 2011, then we would use HD999.C27<u>3</u>, and the second Cutter will represent the region or country (Mexico in our case—M6). Since that takes up our second Cutter slot, we have to use line 5 of the Cutter table to Cutter the first letter of the author's last name if we want to include the author information in the call number (L = 5 on line 5 of the Cutter table):

HD9999.C273 M65 2011
HD9999 = special industries or trades
.C273 = car washes, by region or country
M65 = Mexico (M6) + first letter of the author's last name, L (5)
2011 = date of publication

THE TRANSLATION TABLE

In addition to the many other tables that apply to certain parts of the LCC schedules, there are tables that apply across LCC. One is the Translation Table, which is a special table for translations of a work from one language to another. For example, what if the history of car washes book by Eleanor Lisbeth that we discussed earlier was originally written in Spanish and has been translated into English? Your library owns the English translation and not the Spanish-language original. You simply keep the call number of the original Spanish-language work except for the publication date (that should match the publication date of the translation): HD9999.C272 L57. Then consult the following Translation Table at G150 in the *Classification and Shelflisting Manual* (CSM):

TRANSLATION TABLE	
.x	Original work
.x12	Polyglot (2 or more languages of translation)[*]
.x125	Arabic translation
.x127	Chinese translation
.x13	English translation
.x14	French translation
.x15	German translation
.x154	Hebrew translation
.x16	Italian translation
.x163	Japanese translation
.x164	Korean translation
.x167	Portuguese translation
.x17	Russian translation
.x18	Spanish translation
.x19	Vietnamese translation

[*]*Until 2013, polyglot was defined as 3 or more languages.*

Translation Table

The .x represents the main entry Cutter for the original work. Find the language of the translation and add the numbers following the .x to the end of the main entry Cutter in the translation (English = .x13). Assuming the translation was published in 2013, our call number will be HD9999.C272 L57<u>13</u> 2013. Here is the same call number, but in different translations:

HD9999.C272 L57<u>15</u> 2013 (German translation)
HD9999.C272 L57<u>154</u> 2013 (Hebrew translation)
HD9999.C272 L57<u>163</u> 2013 (Japanese translation)
HD9999.C272 L57<u>17</u> 2013 (Russian translation)

Translations of fiction works are treated differently (we will discuss this in chapter 12), and there are a few other exceptions, according to the CSM G150:

Do not use the Translation Table:

- for entries with a corporate or conference creator
- for serials
- for autobiographies or correspondence
- when using the Biography Table, except for the .xA6–Z area
- when a caption includes the instructions "By date," unless a subarrangement is explicitly printed in the schedules.

THE BIOGRAPHY TABLE

Biographies are works that are about the lives of one or more individuals. *Individual biographies* focus primarily on the life of one individual (for example, a biography of Albert Einstein), whereas *collective biographies* are about the lives of two or more individuals covered in distinct sections (for example, a collection of biographies about popular basketball players in the United States). In LCC, biographies are usually assigned class numbers within the field with which the subject is primarily associated. For example, biographies of Elvis Presley are classed in ML420 (Literature on music, in particular biographies of singers). However, there are exceptions. Biographies about people who are not associated with a particular field are classed in the C schedule (CT, specifically).

Biographies are discussed specifically in CSM G320 (https://www .loc.gov/aba/publications/FreeCSM/G320.pdf). G320 states that it is important to determine as soon as possible if you need to use a "general number" or a "biography number" because this determines whether or not you should use the Biography Table (which I will talk more about in a moment). "General numbers" usually incorporate biographies into a class number rather than having a separate class number or Cutter for them. For example, F73.4, the class number used for Massachusetts local history (early to 1775), should be used to class historical works about this time period in Massachusetts, but also for biographies about people who lived in Massachusetts during this time period (William Blackstone being one example).

On the other hand, "biography numbers" require a separate class number or Cutter number for biographies, for example, GV884, the class number used for collective or individual biographies of basketball players. The Biography Table should be used with these "biography number" class numbers, but only the ones that require the first Cutter to represent the subject of the biography (there are some class numbers where the *second* Cutter represents the subject of the biography—do not apply the Biography Table to these class numbers). Before I say anything further, here is the Biography Table (it can also be found in CSM G320, mentioned above):

BIOGRAPHY TABLE

.x	Cutter for the biographee
.xA2	Collected works. By date
.xA25	Selected works. Selections. By date Including quotations
.xA3	Autobiography, diaries, etc. By date
.xA4	Letters. By date
.xA5	Speeches, essays, and lectures. By date Including interviews
.xA6-Z	Individual biography and criticism. By main entry Including criticism of selected works, autobiography, quotations, letters, speeches, interviews, etc.

In .xA6-Z, do not Cutter lower than A6.   The suggested Cutter numbers for entries beginning with A are:

Aa-Af	A6-699
Ag-Al	A7-799
Am-Ar	A8-899
As-Az	A9-999

Biography Table

Let's use GV884, the class number for collective or individual biographies of basketball players, to demonstrate how the Biography Table should be used. Here is the entry for GV884 in Classification Web:

	Basketball
GV882	Periodicals. Societies. Serials
GV883	History
	Biography
GV884.A1	Collective
GV884.A2-Z	Individual, A-Z

Basketball—GV882 through GV884

Note how collective biographies of basketball players should be assigned GV884.A1. I would assign this class number to the following work: *Basketball Legends* by Paul J. Deegan, published in 1990. The first Cutter represents collective biographies, and the second Cutter should represent the author, Deegan: GV884.A1 D44 1990. However, let's say I am cataloging this biography of an individual basketball player: *Michael Jordan: A Shooting Star* by George Beahm, published in 1994. We still use GV884, but the first Cutter (Individual, A–Z) should represent the individual subject of the biography—in this case, Michael Jordan. This pattern follows the Biography Table, where the lowercase "x" represents the first Cutter ("the Cutter for the biographee"). Therefore, the call number for the Michael Jordan biography above should be

GV884.J67 B43 1994
GV884 = biographies of basketball players
.J67 = Michael Jordan
B43 = the author of the work, Beahm
1994 = date of publication

Looking at the Biography Table more closely, you should see that we can also add a second Cutter to signify that a work is an autobiography (A3), letters (A4), or an interview (A5), in addition to other types, most of which are organized by date. Consequently, if I am cataloging an autobiography of Michael Jordan published in 1999, I would have the following call number:

GV884.J67 A3 1999
GV884 = biographies of basketball players
.J67 = Michael Jordan
A3 = autobiography
1999 = date of publication

The .xA6–Z part of the Biography Table represents the main entry of the work if it is an individual biography or criticism. The *Michael Jordan: A Shooting Star* by George Beahm book that I discussed earlier falls into this category. The information at and below .xA6–Z in the table speaks to the need to Cutter the main entry (in the above example, the main entry is the author, Beahm) so that it is between A6 and Z to ensure it does not conflict with the Cutter for Collected Works (A2) through Speeches, Essays, and Lectures (A5).

It is important to keep in mind that tables are used in special situations and should not be applied to every class number, nor should you apply them in every case. As I demonstrated above, you might find it beneficial to avoid the specificity that some tables provide if it is not needed for your institution's collection. On the other hand, some collections would benefit from more precise call numbers if they contain many resources on the same topic. In the next chapter, I will cover the use of embedded tables in LCC. They contain many of the same structures for number building that we encountered in this chapter, but sometimes with additional instructions as well.

EXERCISES

Construct LCC call numbers for the following works. Feel free to answer with or without MARC coding.

1. A history of the information services industry by Shanna Miksa, published in 1997.
2. A general work on the history of education in Texas by Anna Dover, published in 1980.
3. A history of education in Dallas, Texas, by Victor Espino, published in 1995.

4. A history of railroads in Germany by Felix Zug, published in 2010.
5. A general work on private medical care plans in Poland by Ksenia Pawlak, published in 2015.
6. A work on fraud and swindling in Tokyo, Japan, by Ponzi Abagnale, published in 2000.
7. A work about banana workers in Brazil by Marcos Rocha, published in 2007.

Use the Translation Table to create call numbers for the following translations:

8. The work in question 1 translated into Italian, published in 1999.
9. The work in question 2 translated into Korean, published in 1981.
10. The work in question 3 translated into Arabic, published in 1998.
11. A polyglot translation of the work in question 4, published in 2014.

Use the Biography Table to create call numbers for the following works:

12. An autobiography of ice skater Kristi Yamaguchi, published in 2001.
13. A biography of physicist Albert Einstein by Emma Grimble, published in 1989.
14. A book of Albert Einstein quotations, published in 1966.
15. An interview with rock musician Bruce Springsteen by James Sullivan, published in 1987 (hint: use class number ML420).

Advanced Call Number Building Using Embedded Tables

Embedded tables in LCC are not separately labeled tables like I discussed in the last chapter, but they also contain instructions for more specific call number building. They are included as part of the schedule text. Here is an example of an embedded table at HD3616:

HD3616.A-Z	By region or country, A-Z
	Under each country (except the United States):
.x	Periodicals. Societies. Serials
.x2	History
.x3	Public policy
.x4A-.x4Z	Local, A-Z

HD3616 Embedded Table

Let's walk through another example:

```
The Economic Conditions
       of Illinois


          by


    Cate Sassen
```

The Economic Conditions of Illinois

You are cataloging the above book on the current economic conditions of the state of Illinois by Cate Sassen, published in 2016.

HC107 is the class number that represents the economic history and conditions of various geographic areas of the United States (regions, states, counties, etc.):

HC107.A19	Pacific Northwest
HC107.A195	Columbia River Valley
HC107.A2-.W	Individual states, A-W
	For list of Cutter numbers for individual states (except those listed below), see Table H28
	Under each state:
	.x General works
	.x2A-.x2Z By region, county, parish, A-Z
	.x3A-.x3Z Special topics, A-Z
	For list of topics, see HC79
HC107.S7	South Carolina
HC107.T3	Tennessee
HC107.W5	West Virginia
HC107.W9	Wyoming

HC107—Economic Conditions of US States

Before we get to the embedded table (located below "Under each state"), let's determine the call number for the example item above using what we already know about tables. Our class number will be HC107, and if possible we should try to include the fact that the work is about the current economic conditions of Illinois specifically. According to the caption for HC107, the first Cutter after HC107 should represent the individual US state ("Individual states, A–W"). That Cutter should be between A2 and W according to the Cutters after HC107 on the left. Why A2 through W? A2 begins the range because LCC has already assigned Cutters A11 through A195 to specific *regions* in the United States. The end of the range is W because there is no US state that begins with a letter past W— that is, X, Y, or Z.

Note the instruction below the caption "Individual states, A–W": "For list of Cutter numbers for individual states (except those listed below), see Table H28." This is the type of table we have encountered before, but it looks slightly different. Table H28 contains a list of Cutters representing specific states in the United States. Clicking on the hyperlinked H28 takes you to the beginning of the table (you can see more states by clicking on the right arrow [>] on the page):

Table of states (Cutter number)

Table of states (Cutter number)	
H28 .A2	Alabama
H28 .A4	Alaska
H28 .A6	Arizona
H28 .A8	Arkansas
H28 .C2	California
H28 .C6	Colorado
H28 .C8	Connecticut
H28 .D3	Delaware
H28 .F6	Florida
H28 .G4	Georgia
H28 .H3	Hawaii
H28 .I2	Idaho
H28 .I3	Illinois
H28 .I6	Indiana
H28 .I8	Iowa
H28 .K2	Kansas
H28 .K4	Kentucky

Table H28—US States

In place of a class number, the table number H28 is used. The Cutter represents a specific state (.A2 = Alabama, .H3 = Hawaii, etc.). Take the applicable state Cutter from this table and apply it to HC107, but note the "exceptions" listed at HC107: South Carolina, Tennessee, West Virginia, and Wyoming. For some reason, the Cutter numbers given after HC107 for these states do not match the ones listed in Table H28. However, our work is about Illinois, which is represented by Cutter .I3 in Table H28.

Now, let's go back to HC107 and discuss the rest of the entry, namely, the embedded table:

Under each state:

.x	General works
.x2A-.x2Z	By region, county, parish, A-Z
.x3A-.x3Z	Special topics, A-Z
	For list of topics, see HC79

HC107 Embedded Table

We discussed the meaning of the lowercase "x" in the last chapter; it is a placeholder for the first Cutter, which in this case should be the Cutter for the individual US state. For general works on the economic history and conditions of an individual state, include the Cutter for the individual US state after HC107, Cutter the main entry, and add the publication date as usual. Therefore, our work on the current economic conditions of the state of Illinois by Cate Sassen, published in 2016, should have this call number (assuming we don't need to adjust the main entry Cutter due to shelflist issues):

HC107.I3 S27 2016
HC107 = economic history and conditions of US states or regions
.I3 = Illinois
S27 = the main entry (Sassen)
2016 = publication date

This is fairly straightforward, but what about the .x2A–.x2Z and .x3A–.x3Z? These should be consulted if you are cataloging a work on a particular region, county, or parish within a US state, or if the work is about a specific economic topic that applies to a particular state, like consumer protection in California or economic development projects in Georgia. However, let's take this one step at a time and explore .x2A–.x2Z for regions, counties, and parishes first.

Going back to our previous example, let's assume that Cate Sassen's book is actually about the economic conditions of Cook County, Illinois, specifically and not about Illinois generally. According to LCC, if we want to include the county information, we need to follow this formula: .x2A–.x2Z. The lowercase "x" represents the first Cutter, which in this example should be .I3 for Illinois. The formula then says that we should add a "2" to the end of the first Cutter to signify that our next Cutter represents a specific region, county, or parish as opposed to the second Cutter representing the main entry. Therefore, we add a "2" to the end of the Illinois Cutter (.I32). "A" and "Z" represent the second Cutter: the region, county, or parish. It should fit between A and Z. Our example book is about Cook County, which is Cuttered C6 and fits easily between A and Z. Since Cook County takes up the second Cutter slot, we have to use line 5 of the Cutter table to Cutter the first letter of the author's name (S = 7) and add it to the end of the second Cutter. Here is the breakdown:

HC107 .I32 C67 2016

HC107 = economic history and conditions of US states or regions

.I32 = Illinois + "2" signifying that the second Cutter represents a region, county, or parish and *not* the main entry

C67 = Cook County (C6) + "7" ("S" from line 5 of the Cutter table from the author's last name, Sassen)

2016 = date of publication

The next part of the embedded table, .x3A–.x3Z, is a little different from what we have encountered before. As I mentioned previously, .x3A–.x3Z is used for works on special economic topics, which the table mentions are listed at class number HC79. Use the Cutters provided at HC79 to build your call number that begins with HC107. In this particular instance, the use of aspects from both HC79 and HC107 allows us to create a call number about a special economic topic within a particular US state. Let's say that Cate Sassen wrote another book in 2016 about the flow of funds in Illinois.

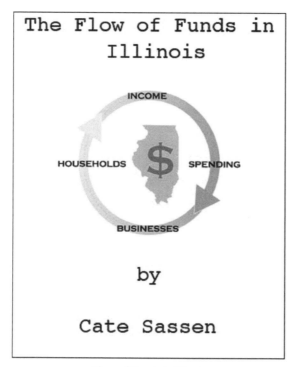

Flow of Funds in Illinois

LCC instructs you to go to HC79 for a list of special topics:

Under each state:
.x   General works
.x2A-.x2Z   By region, county, parish, A-Z
.x3A-.x3Z   Special topics, A-Z
                    For list of topics, see <u>HC79</u>

HC107 Embedded Table—HC79 Highlighted

HC79 is hyperlinked, so click on it and you should see this screen:

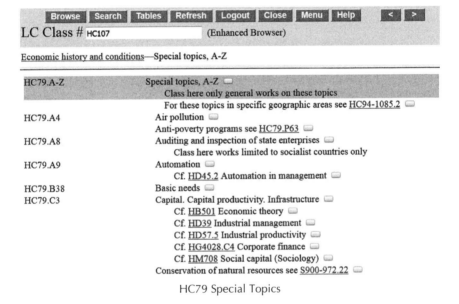

HC79 Special Topics

If you click on the right arrow (>), you will eventually find "Flow of funds" at HC79.F55:

Flow of Funds—HC79 .F55

At this point, we want to treat HC79 like it is a table, even though it is not—it is an LCC class number. What we want from HC79 is the *Cutter* after HC79 representing flow of funds (.F55) because we already know that we want to use the class number HC107. We do not want to use HC79 as the class number because it does not allow you to include a Cutter for a geographic place. More on this in a moment.

Take the flow of funds Cutter (.F55) and return back to the embedded table at HC107. Within .x3A–.x3Z, the lowercase "x" still represents the US state (Illinois in our case—.I3). Instead of adding a "2" to the end of the first Cutter like we did before, we add a "3" (.I33) to signify that the second Cutter represents a special topic, and that special topic Cutter should be between A and Z (flow of funds = F55). Add a number from line 5 of the Cutter table representing the main entry, Sassen (7), and the publication year. Here, again, is the breakdown:

HC107 .I33 F557 2016
HC107 = economic history and conditions of US states or regions
.I33 = Illinois (.I3) + "3" signifying that the second Cutter represents a special topic and *not* the main entry
F557 = flow of funds (F55 from HC79) + "7" from line 5 of the Cutter table, representing the author, Sassen
2016 = date of publication

As an aside, it is very likely that you would begin your search for "flow of funds" not at HC107 (unless you are well versed in the ins and outs of this particular class number!), but by searching for "flow of funds":

LC Classification Search

Caption ❶	Flow of funds
Keyword ❶	
Index term ❶	
Caption or index term ❶	
Classification number ❶	

Search tips and options

LC Classification Search—Flow of Funds

If you perform a caption search for "flow of funds," you receive HC79
.F55 as a result, as we know from our previous investigation:

LC Classification Search: Caption

Flow of funds (1)
    HC79.F55   Flow of funds ▭

Flow of funds accounting (1)
    HB142.5   Flow of funds accounting ▭

Flow of gases in pipes. Air meters (1)
    [TJ1025-1030]   Flow of gases in pipes. Air meters ▭

Flow of liquids (1)
    TP156.F6   Flow of liquids ▭

Flow of Funds Caption Search Result

If you go to the beginning of HC79 (click on "Special topics, A–Z" in the
breadcrumbs when you go to HC79.F55), you will see this:

Economic history and conditions—Special topics, A-Z

HC79.A-Z	Special topics, A-Z ▭
	Class here only general works on these topics
	For these topics in specific geographic areas see HC94-1085.2 ▭
HC79.A4	Air pollution ▭
	Anti-poverty programs see HC79.P63 ▭
HC79.A8	Auditing and inspection of state enterprises ▭
	Class here works limited to socialist countries only
HC79.A9	Automation ▭
	Cf. HD45.2 Automation in management ▭
HC79.B38	Basic needs ▭

Beginning of HC79 Special Topics

Note the instruction under the caption that says, "For these topics
in specific geographic areas see HC94–1085.2." This will take you to
HC107, which allows you to include not only the special topic, but a
geographic place if you want to include both attributes. You cannot
simply add a geographic Cutter to HC79. You can add special topic and

geographic Cutters only when they are included in the schedules or when you are instructed to do so.

Tables (embedded or otherwise) are used regularly in LCC. They are intimidating at first, but they often follow a similar pattern, so once you get comfortable using them they are fairly easy to interpret. In addition, it is not uncommon to find that both Cutter "slots" are taken by topic or geographic Cutters. If it is unlikely that your institution will add further works on the same topic, then it may be fine to leave out main entry information. On the other hand, we cannot always predict the future, so adding another number to the end of the second Cutter to represent the main entry is good practice to avoid future confusion and conflicts.

EXERCISE

Construct LCC call numbers for the following works. Feel free to answer with or without MARC coding.

1. A general work on art study in universities and colleges in Rhode Island by Arnold King, published in 1983.
2. A work on murder in France, specifically in the city of Paris, by Tristan Guibord, published in 2002. Hint: perform a keyword search for murder by region or country.
3. A work on labor productivity in Florida by Agostina Riva, published in 1975.
4. A work on planetariums in Phoenix, Arizona, by Gina Stargazer, probably published in 1942.
5. The study and teaching of dairying in Dairyland, Wisconsin, by Tom Leche, published in 1989.

12

Classifying Fiction in LCC

For most items you classify using LCC, choose the class number based on the subject matter of the work. However, LCC treats literature, such as fiction, poetry, and drama, differently. When the author of the work is known, class the work by the name of the author.

LCC divides Literature (class P) by nationality (American, English, Slavic, Italian, etc.) and time period of the author (when the author lived and/or was productive, *not* necessarily when their works were published). For example, English fiction is classed in PR and American fiction is classed in PS. Here is a screenshot of the PR schedule:

Browse Search Tables Refresh Logout Close Menu Help < >	
LC Class # PR	(Hierarchy Browser)

English literature—Literary history and criticism

PR1-56	Literary history and criticism
PR57-78	Criticism
	Cf. PN80-99 General literary criticism
PR80.2-990	History of English literature
PR1098-1369.23	Collections of English literature
PR1490-1799.2	Anglo-Saxon literature
	Anglo-Norman period. Early English. Middle English
PR2199-3195.22	English renaissance (1500-1640)
PR3291-3785	17th and 18th centuries (1640-1770)
PR3991-5990	19th century. 1770/1800-1890/1900
PR6000-6049	1900-1960
	Including usually authors beginning to publish about 1890, flourishing after 1900
	For works of fiction cataloged before July 1, 1980, except limited editions and works in the Rare Book Collection see PZ3-4
PR6050-6076	1961-2000
	Including usually authors beginning to publish about 1950, flourishing after 1960
	For works of fiction cataloged before July 1, 1980, except limited editions and works in the Rare Book Collection see PZ4
PR6100-6126	2001-
PR8309-9680	English literature: Provincial, local, etc.
	Class here literary history, collected biography and collections of the

PR Class

Note the ranges of class numbers by time period. English authors who published during the years 1900–1960 will be classed between PR6000 and PR6049. Authors who lived or were productive prior to the twentieth century are assigned a specific class number or class number range that catalogers use to class his or her works. For example, class numbers PR2750 through PR3112 are reserved for William Shakespeare. Post-twentieth-century authors are assigned a class number based on the first letter of their last name, plus a Cutter representing the specific author. For example, the call numbers for Stephen King's works begin with PS3561.I483. Biographies of that author and criticisms of his or her works are classed with works by the author as well. If the specific author you are looking for is not listed in LCC, you can create a call number that places that author alphabetically between authors already listed. I will talk more about what to do if you cannot find a particular author in LCC later on in this chapter.

Let's work through an example. Let's say you are cataloging this work of fiction: *The Hound of the Baskervilles* by Sir Arthur Conan Doyle, published in 2001:

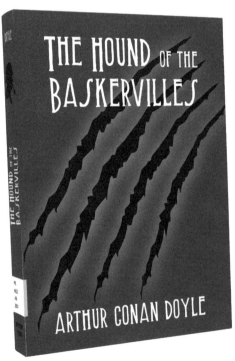

The Hound of the Baskervilles

Where do you start? As I mentioned earlier, you don't have to worry about determining the subject matter of the work. Once you have determined it is fiction, you need to locate the name of the author. The author of this work is nineteenth-century English author Sir Arthur Conan Doyle. If you don't know the author's nationality and/or the time period in which he or she wrote, it is always a good idea to do a little outside research to learn at least this basic information about the author. Your next step is searching for the author's name in the LC Classification Search. Don't search for the name in the normal order (Arthur Conan Doyle). Instead, invert the name, putting the surname first and the forename (and any middle names) second (Doyle, Arthur Conan).

When I type "Doyle, Arthur Conan" into the caption search, I get this result:

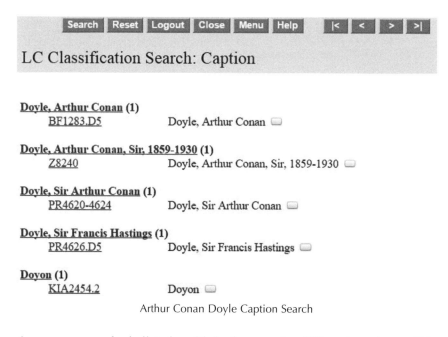

Arthur Conan Doyle Caption Search

As you can see, he is listed multiple times under different versions of his name. This is not entirely uncommon since the Library of Congress does not always update names to the preferred forms if they change. However, as long as we stay focused, we can find the correct class number despite these confusing results. The first Doyle is at BF1383.D5, the second at Z8240, and the third at PR4620–4624. We could click on each of these to see which one is most appropriate, but recall our discussion about how English literature is in class PR. With this in mind, your best bet is the third result: PR4620–4624. We can double-check this choice by examining the authority record for Arthur Conan Doyle, the document that contains his preferred form of name, variant forms of his name, and other identifying information. You can look at the Library of Congress's authority records for free by going to http://authorities.loc.gov. Here is a portion of Doyle's authority record on the LC Authorities website:

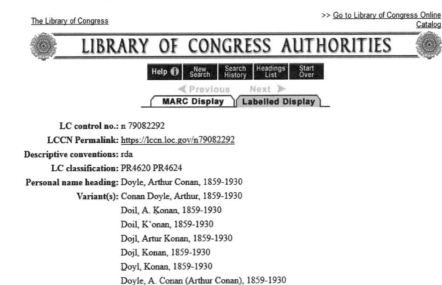

Arthur Conan Doyle Authority Record

Many literature author authority records contain LC classification information that should at least give you an idea of the area of LCC where you should focus your attention. In the "LC classification" field (MARC field 053), there is PR4620 and PR4624. This field does not give you enough information to build a complete call number, but it does tell you where to start.

If we go back to Doyle's search results in Classification Web, we see the same PR4620–4624 range. Click on it:

Arthur Conan Doyle Caption Search—PR Result Highlighted

When you click on PR4620–4624, you should see this screen:

PR4620–4624—Doyle, Arthur Conan

Always make sure to note the breadcrumbs at the top of the page to ensure that you are in the right place in the schedules. If your breadcrumbs don't seem right, you need to search again. Also note that Arthur Conan

Doyle's name (highlighted above) is hyperlinked because a table (Table P–PZ35) is applicable here. If you click on his hyperlinked name, this will show you further options for classifying works by and about him, just as we did when we looked at tables in the last few chapters. When you click on the hyperlink, you should see these results:

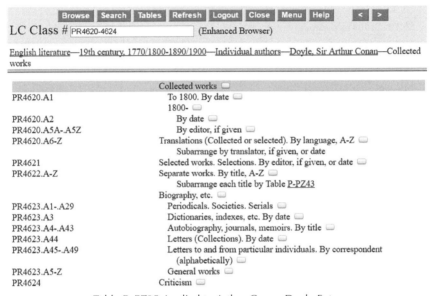

Table P–PZ35 Applied to Arthur Conan Doyle Entry

By clicking on Doyle's name, you have expanded his range of class numbers (PR4620–4624). All of the class numbers you see in the screenshot apply to Doyle, starting with his collected works at PR4620.A1 and ending at criticisms of his work at PR4624. The work we want to classify, *The Hound of the Baskervilles*, is a separate work, as opposed to a collected or selected work. *Collected works* contain the body of an author's work, such as all fiction works, poetry, drama, and so forth (not including correspondence). *Selected works* contain selections of the body of an author's work (it could contain two or hundreds of titles within one work, depending on the output of the author!). *Separate works* are individually published titles.

It is odd to see "To 1800" and "1800–" under "Collected works" since Doyle was born in 1859 (and, as far as I know, did not own a time machine!) and could not have works published before 1800. But keep in mind that the captions and Cutters are from a table (Table P–PZ35, specifically) that is applied across the P class. Every entry in the table may not apply to every author. Here are some examples of call numbers for the collected works of Doyle:

The Collected Works of Arthur Conan Doyle, published in 1970
PR4620 .A2 1970
PR4620 = the collected works of Arthur Conan Doyle
.A2 = organized by date
1970 = publication date

Arthur Conan Doyle's Collected Works, edited by Joan Watson, published in 1994
PR4620 .A5 W3 1994
PR4620 = the collected works of Arthur Conan Doyle
.A5 = organized by editor
W3 = Cutter for the editor, Watson
1994 = publication date

Selected works are classed at PR4621 and organized by editor, if given, or by date. Here is an example of a selected work and its call number (exclude the editor Cutter if not given):

The Selected Works of Arthur Conan Doyle, edited by Jimmy Moriarty, published in 1981
PR4621 .M6 1981

The Hound of the Baskervilles contains only one work and is therefore a separate work and should be classified at PR4622. I used a rectangle to highlight this entry below:

PR4620.A5A-.A5Z	By editor, if given
PR4620.A6-Z	Translations (Collected or selected). By language, A-Z
	Subarrange by translator, if given, or date
PR4621	Selected works. Selections. By editor, if given, or date
PR4622.A-Z	Separate works. By title, A-Z
	Subarrange each title by Table P-PZ43
	Biography, etc.
PR4623.A1-.A29	Periodicals. Societies. Serials
PR4623.A3	Dictionaries, indexes, etc. By date
PR4623.A4-.A43	Autobiography, journals, memoirs. By title
PR4623.A44	Letters (Collections). By date

PR4622 Separate Works Highlighted

Note that the caption says, "Separate works. By title." This means that we should organize an author's separate works by the title of the work. The first Cutter within the call number should represent the title of the work. Also note that there is another table we should consult: Table P–PZ43. If you click on the hyperlinked P–PZ43, you will see this:

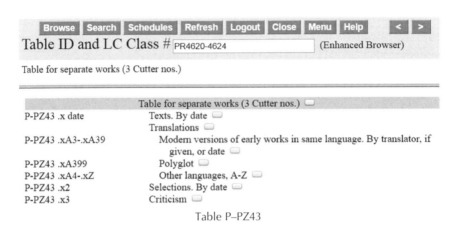

Table P–PZ43

Treat this table like any other table and recall what we discussed over the last few chapters. We can ignore the P–PZ43 on the left-hand side, and we know that the lowercase "x" is a placeholder for the first Cutter (representing the title of the work). The first entry, "P–PZ43 .x date," means that separate works are organized first by the title Cutter (represented by the "x") and then by the date of publication. This will be the case for all separate works except for translations of the separate works (the second Cutter will be A3 through Z, depending on the type of translation), selections of separate works (the title Cutter will have a "2" at the end and then be organized further by date of publication), or a criticism of the separate work (the title Cutter will have a "3" at the end). Since our example work does not fall under any of these categories, we need to move on to the next step: Cuttering the title of the work.

The Hound of the Baskervilles begins with the initial article "The." If you recall from the chapter on Cuttering main entries, ignore initial articles and begin Cuttering the first word after the initial article, which is "Hound" in this case. Use the LCC Cutter Number Generating Table to Cutter "Hound" only one letter past the initial "H" (.H6). It is common for title Cutters to be shorter than main entry Cutters unless there is a reason to extend them further. It is important to double-check your shelflist to see if your institution has other publications of the same work to ensure that all copies use the same Cutter for the title.

Add .H6 after the class number for Doyle's separate works:

PR4622 .H6

We are not instructed at PR4622 to add any further Cutters, so we can simply add the publication date to the call number and we are done:

PR4622 .H6 2001

Do not add a Cutter for the author's last name because it would be redundant. Remember: PR4622 is only for the separate works by Sir Arthur Conan Doyle.

Next I want to create a call number for a fiction work written by an author who *did not* live prior to the twentieth century: Anne Rice, an American author.

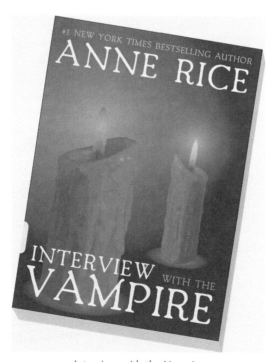

Interview with the Vampire

We will create a call number for *Interview with the Vampire* by Anne Rice, published in 1977. Just like we did with *The Hound of the Baskervilles*, start by searching for Anne Rice, name inverted. You will receive this result:

Rice, Anne, 1941- (1)
PS3568.I265   Rice, Anne, 1941- ▭

Anne Rice Caption Search Result

There is only one result, and PS is American literature, so PS3568.I265 is promising. As I mentioned previously, post-twentieth-century authors will not have their own class number(s). Instead, the class number is based on the first letter of their last name, and the first Cutter represents the specific author. When you click on PS3568.I265, you will see this:

| Browse | Search | Tables | Refresh | Logout | Close | Menu | Help | < | > |

LC Class # PS3568.I265   (Enhanced Browser)

American literature—Individual authors—1961-2000—R—Rice, Anne, 1941-

PS3568.E895	Reynolds, Mack Table P-PZ40 ▭
	Rhoades, Jonathan see PS3565.L77 ▭
PS3568.I265	Rice, Anne, 1941- Table P-PZ40 ▭
PS3568.I35156	Richmond, Leigh Table P-PZ40 ▭
PS3568.I3518	Richmond, Walt Table P-PZ40 ▭
	Ridgeway, Jason, 1928- see PS3563.A674 ▭
	Rikki, 1943- see PS3554.U279 ▭
	Ringo, Clay, 1908- see PS3558.O3473 ▭
PS3568.O198	Robb, Candace M. Table P-PZ40 ▭
	Roberts, Gillian, 1939- see PS3557.R356 ▭
	Roberts, Janet Louise see PS3552.R656 ▭

PS3568.I265 Anne Rice

Just like we did with Doyle, click on the hyperlinked Anne Rice entry, which incorporates Table P–PZ40 into her class number and Cutter:

| Browse | Search | Tables | Refresh | Logout | Close | Menu | Help | < | > |

LC Class # [PS3568.I265]   (Enhanced Browser)

American literature—Individual authors—1961-2000—R—Rice, Anne, 1941-—Collected works

	Collected works ▭
	Including collected works in specific genres
PS3568.I265 date	By date ▭
(PS3568.I265A11-.I265A13)	By editor ▭
	Subarrangement by editor has been discontinued by the Library of Congress.
	Beginning in 2005, all collected works are subarranged by date
(PS3568.I265A14-.I265A19)	Collected prose, poetry, plays, etc. ▭
	For collected genres see P-PZ40 _x date_
	Translations (Collected or selected) ▭
PS3568.I265A199	Modern versions of early authors in the same language. By date ▭
PS3568.I265A1995	Polyglot. By date ▭
PS3568.I265A2	English. By date ▭
PS3568.I265A3	French. By date ▭
PS3568.I265A4	German. By date ▭
PS3568.I265A5-.I265A59	Other. By language (alphabetically) and date ▭
PS3568.I265A6	Selected works. Selections. By date ▭
PS3568.I265A61-.I265Z458	Separate works. By title ▭
	Biography and criticism ▭
PS3568.I265Z4581-.I265Z4589	Periodicals. Societies. Serials ▭
PS3568.I265Z459	Dictionaries, indexes, etc. By date ▭
PS3568.I265Z46	Autobiography, journals, memoirs. By date ▭
PS3568.I265Z48	Letters (Collections). By date ▭
	Including collections of letters to and from particular individuals
PS3568.I265Z5-.I265Z999	General works ▭

Table P–PZ40 Applied to Anne Rice Entry

Except for the class numbers and Cutters on the left-hand side, much of what you see in the caption area should look familiar. The table we applied to Doyle (Table P–PZ35) is not the same as the one we applied to Rice (Table P–PZ40), but they are similar in many ways. Since *Interview with the Vampire* is a separate work like *The Hound of the Baskervilles*, we can focus our attention on the entry for separate works:

PS3568.I265A61-.I265Z458   Separate works. By title ▭

Anne Rice Separate Works Entry

What is the meaning of this great mishmash of numbers and letters? Part of getting comfortable with LCC is looking at the mishmash without running away screaming so we can recognize the same patterns we have explored previously. The first part of what is on the left-hand side is the class number and Cutter we saw previously that represents Anne Rice (PS3568.I265):

PS3568.I265A61-.I265Z458   Separate works. By title ▭

PS3568.I265 Highlighted

All works by and about her, as well as criticisms of her works, begin with PS3568.I265. A61 and Z458 represent the range for the second Cutter; .I265 is repeated before Z458 to emphasize the range of Cutters. The reason why A61 and Z458 were chosen over the more simple A–Z is because Cutters before A61 and after Z458 are taken by other topics (for example, A4 is the second Cutter for German translations of collected or selected works by Anne Rice; Z48 for collected letters). Therefore, we have to make sure that our title Cutter fits between A61 and Z458, which is a simple enough task for most titles.

The Cutter for *Interview* is I5 (following the same Cuttering pattern we used on *Hounds*). Even though it doesn't state it explicitly, we can add the publication date as well:

PS3568.I265 I5 1977
PS3568 = American literature authors who lived or were productive between 1961 and 2000 whose last names begin with "R"
.I265 = works by and about Anne Rice, including criticisms
I5 = Cutter for the separate work, *Interview with the Vampire*
1977 = publication date

Authors who are not listed in Classification Web should be assigned a class number and Cutter based on where they would file normally. For example, twentieth-century American author William Faulkner is not listed with other American authors whose last name begins with "F":

PS3511.A738	Farrell, James T. (James Thomas), 1904-1979
	Fast, Govard see PS3511.A784
PS3511.A784	Fast, Howard, 1914-
	Fast, Khauard see PS3511.A784
PS3511.A87	Faust, Frederick, 1892-1944
	Feikema, Feike see PS3525.A52233
	Feikema, Frederick see PS3525.A52233
PS3511.E56	Fernald, Chester Bailey Table P-PZ40
	Fever, Buck see PS3501.N4
	Field, Peter, 1900- see PS3535.E745
PS3511.I557	Finger, Charles Joseph, 1869-1941 Table P-PZ40

Twentieth-Century American Authors—Last Name Beginning with "F"

Alphabetically, Faulkner should fit between Howard Fast (PS3511.A784) and Frederick Faust (PS3511.A87), so we could pick a Cutter between .A784 and .A87 that is not already taken. Or we can check Faulkner's authority record in http://authorities.loc.gov first!

LIBRARY OF CONGRESS AUTHORITIES

| Help | New Search | Search History | Headings List | Start Over |

◀ Previous   **Next** ▶

MARC Display   Labelled Display

LC control no.: n 79003304
LCCN Permalink: https://lccn.loc.gov/n79003304
Descriptive conventions: rda
LC classification: PS3511.A86
Personal name heading: Faulkner, William, 1897-1962
Variant(s): Falkner, William, 1897-1962
Fōkunā, Wiriamu, 1897-1962
Folkner, Uil'iam, 1897-1962
Fo-k'o-na, 1897-1962
Phōkner, Ouilliam, 1897-1962
Fo-k'o-na, Wei-lien, 1897-1962
Fu-k'o-na, 1897-1962
Fu-k'o-na, Wei-lien, 1897-1962

William Faulkner Authority Record

According to his authority record, the Library of Congress uses PS3511 .A86. This doesn't necessarily mean you *have to* use the same Cutter, but it is often helpful to be consistent with the Library of Congress for copy cataloging purposes. I recommend checking an author's authority record first before you go through the motions of creating a Cutter from scratch.

Let's move from literature by one author to collections of literature by different authors. These works typically are classed first by nationality and then by either type of literature (poetry, drama, etc.), place, time period, or special topic. American adventure stories, for example, are classed at PS509.A3. You can class collections of English literature published before 1801 at PR1101 and after 1801 at PR1105. To see the many ways you can class literature, I recommend browsing LCC using the Outline I mention in chapter 7 ("Browsing LCC in Classification Web").

If you are used to libraries organizing their collections by genre, LCC's system of organizing mainly by nationality, time period, and author may seem strange and overwhelming. But there are benefits to organizing fiction in this way: all (or most) works by and about an author and his or her works can be found in one place, regardless of genre or type of literature. In addition, authors receive unique call numbers that are hard to obtain in Dewey Decimal Classification and bookstore-style organizational systems.

EXERCISE

Construct LCC call numbers for the following works without worrying about how the call number might fit in an existing shelflist. Feel free to answer with or without MARC coding.

1. *The Jungle Book*, a novel by British author Rudyard Kipling, published in 1965.
2. *Sphere*, a novel by American author Michael Crichton, published in 1999.
3. *The Grass Is Singing*, a novel by British author Doris Lessing, published in 2008.
4. *Americana*, a novel by American author Don DeLillo, published in 1989.
5. *Stardust*, a novel by British American author Neil Gaiman, published in 1997.
6. *Ficciones*, the selected works of Argentinean author Jorge Luis Borges, edited by Huberto Rubio, published in 1962.
7. The collected works of Lewis Carroll (pseudonym of Charles Lutwidge Dodgson), published in 1951 (no editor given).

13

Other Avenues and Resources

Now that we have reached the end of our short LCC journey, I want to discuss some alternate ways to find LCC class numbers and resources that will help you dig deeper. This book has only scratched the surface of Library of Congress Classification, but I hope it has given you a good foundation on which to build.

Classification Web provides a wealth of resources to help you locate classification numbers. The Bibliographic Correlations tool, accessible from the main menu of Classification Web, provides a way to locate equivalent (or closely equivalent) LC class numbers if you have already determined the Library of Congress Subject Heading (LCSH), Dewey Decimal Classification number, National Library of Medicine (NLM) classification number, or creator of the work (in the case of literature works). Here is a screenshot of the Bibliographic Correlations search screen in Classification Web:

| Search | Reset | Logout | Close | Menu | Help |

Correlations Search

Search text [   ]

Search type

| LC class number => Dewey class number | ▲ | 25 records per page ▼ |
| LC class number => NLM class number |
| LC class number => LC subject heading |
| LC class number => LC subject heading (including names) |
| **LC subject heading => LC class number** |
| LC subject heading => Dewey class Number |
| LC subject heading => NLM class number |
| LC subject heading (including names) => LC class number |
| LC subject heading (including names) => Dewey class Number |
| LC subject heading (including names) => NLM class number |
| Name as Creator (1xx field) => LC Class Number |
| Name as Creator (1xx field) => Dewey Class Number |
| Name as Creator (1xx field) => NLM Class Number |
| Dewey class number => LC class number |
| Dewey class number => LC subject heading |
| Dewey class number => LC subject heading (including names) |
| NLM class number => LC class number |
| NLM class number => LC subject heading |
| NLM class number => LC subject heading (including names) | ▼ |

Correlations Search Screen

For example, if you have determined an appropriate LCSH for the work you are cataloging and would like to know which LC classification numbers are associated with that subject heading in LC's catalog, choose the LCSH → LC class number search type, type in the LCSH, and press Enter. If there is a correlation, you will see a list of LC class numbers associated with that heading. The number in parentheses next to the class number signifies how many records in LC's catalog use that LCSH/LC class number combination.

In addition, Classification Web often includes LCC numbers with entries in the LCSH list. Considering that the LCC call number should be based on the first-listed subject heading in a record, finding the appropriate LCSH first (assuming you are using LCSH!) can save you a lot of time searching for an LC class number.

The LCC numbers included in LCSH within Classification Web are hyperlinked, so you can click on one and it will take you to that entry in LCC within Classification Web. Here is the LC Subject Heading "Africanized honeybee" in LCSH and the correlating LCC numbers underneath the heading:

Africanized honeybee (May Subd Geog)
[QL568.A6 (Zoology)]
[SF538.5.A37 (Pest)]
[SF539.5-.6 (Culture)]
> UF African-Brazilian honeybee
> African killer bee
> Africanized bee
> Africanized Brazilian honeybee
> Apis mellifera adansonii
> Apis mellifera scutelata
> Brazilian bee
> Brazilian honeybee [Former heading]

Africanized Honeybee Subject Heading with LCC Numbers

Once again, knowing about this alternate route to LCC can be helpful when you are struggling to find a topic directly in LCC.

And don't forget about another way of finding an LCC number that I discussed in chapter 12 on classifying fiction works. You can search for the authority records for LCSHs on the LC Authorities website (http://authorities.loc.gov). Often these authority records include at least a starting point for constructing an LCC call number. Appropriate LCC numbers will be in the element labeled "LC classification" (MARC field 053).

LC control no.: sh 85016614
LCCN Permalink: https://lccn.loc.gov/sh85016614
LC classification: QL568.A6 Zoology
SF538.5.A37 Pest
SF539.5 SF539.6 Culture
Topical subject heading: Africanized honeybee
Variant(s): African-Brazilian honeybee
African killer bee
Africanized bee
Africanized Brazilian honeybee
Apis mellifera adansonii
Apis mellifera scutelata

Africanized Honeybee Authority Record

Currently, OCLC has a free, experimental classification service that provides an alternate means of generating LCC numbers. At this website, http://classify.oclc.org/classify2, you can enter a standard number (such as ISBN), a title and/or author, or a FAST (Faceted Application of Subject Terminology) subject heading, and OCLC will attempt to find frequently assigned Dewey and Library of Congress class numbers (not full call numbers at this time). This service, used in conjunction with your own local catalog, is an excellent means of locating LCC numbers applicable to works on certain topics. When I had to construct an LCC call number for works on topics I knew nothing about and had trouble finding in LCC, I often browsed similar titles in the catalog and on the web to see what subject headings and classification numbers were assigned. There is no one "correct" way of finding an LCC number. What is important is knowing the many resources and methods that can help you assign an LCC call number of which you can be proud!

Here is a list of the resources I referenced throughout this book, as well as a few more that should help you learn more about Library of Congress Classification:

Library of Congress. Classification Web—http://classificationweb.net
A subscription-based resource that contains not only the LCC schedules and tables, but other cataloging resources, such as Library of Congress Subject Headings. It also contains the Bibliographic Correlations tool that can provide LCC numbers that correspond to specific Dewey Decimal Classification numbers and Library of Congress Subject Headings.

Library of Congress. PDFs of Library of Congress Classification—https://www.loc.gov/aba/publications/FreeLCC/freelcc.html
PDFs of the LCC schedules and tables that are free to access but lack the functionality of LCC in Classification Web.

Library of Congress. *Classification and Shelflisting Manual* (CSM)—https://www.loc.gov/aba/publications/FreeCSM/freecsm.html
Library of Congress's guide to LCC. It contains information on the general principles of classification, Cuttering instructions, and guidelines for classifying different types of resources. You can also access CSM through

Cataloger's Desktop (https://desktop.loc.gov) if your institution has a subscription to it.

Library of Congress Authorities—http://authorities.loc.gov
Free, web-based authority file containing authority records for names, subjects, and titles. Many of these records contain LCC numbers as well.

Kyle Banerjee's Cataloging Calculator—http://calculate.alptown.com
A free, web-based tool for creating Cutter numbers and so much more.

OCLC. Classify—http://classify.oclc.org/classify2
Provides LCC and Dewey Decimal Classification numbers corresponding to specific standard numbers (such as an ISBN), titles, authors, and FAST subject headings in WorldCat.

Broughton, V. (2015). *Essential Classification*, 2nd edition. Chicago: Neal-Schuman.
Broughton takes a broader view of classification (including subject headings) but includes several chapters on classifying using LCC.

Chan, L. M., Intner, S. S., and Weihs, J. (2016). *Guide to the Library of Congress Classification*, 6th edition. Santa Barbara, CA: Libraries Unlimited.
Comprehensive and in-depth coverage of the history and principles of LCC, as well as the methods of classifying all areas of LCC.

EXERCISES

1. Which LCC number is associated with the LCSH "Digital cameras"?
2. Which LCC number is associated with the LCSH "Linked data"?
3. What range of LCC numbers should you use for works on dude ranches?
4. LCSH "Apples" is associated with which LCC numbers?
5. You are cataloging a work on "Tea," but the focus is on tea customs. If you look up "Tea" in LCSH, which LCC numbers are associated with tea customs?

6. Is there an LCC number associated with the LCSH "Trees—Identification"? If not, what other ways can we determine an LCC number
   for this topic other than searching directly in LCC?

7. Use the Bibliographic Correlations tool to find the most common
   LCC number used with the following LCSHs:

   a. Unicorns
   b. Timing circuits
   c. Dating (Social customs)
   d. Cats—Behavior
   e. Impressionism (Art)—France

Answers to End-of-Chapter Exercises

CHAPTER 1: LIBRARY OF CONGRESS CLASSIFICATION IN A NUTSHELL

1. LCC has how many main classes? **21**
2. What does the Library of Congress use to justify the creation, deletion, or modification of class numbers? **Literary warrant**
3. What are the three main parts of an LCC call number? **The class number, the Cutter, and the date**
4. What is the name of the online, subscription-based resource produced by the Library of Congress that allows you to search and browse Library of Congress Classification? **Classification Web**
5. What online resource is the Library of Congress's guide to LCC? **The *Classification and Shelflisting Manual* (CSM)**

CHAPTER 2: DATES

1. The item you are cataloging was published in 1981. What year should you include in the call number for this work? **1981**
2. The item you are cataloging was published in 2001, with a copyright date of 2000. What year should you include in the call number for this work? **2001—you can put only one date at the end of the call number. Prefer the publication date.**

3. You think the item you are cataloging was published in 1959, but it is questionable. In 264_1$c you put [1959?]. How should you transcribe the date in the call number for this item? **1959—even uncertain publication dates can be added to the call number. Don't forget to exclude the additional characters, such as the question mark and square brackets!**

4. You are cataloging a facsimile reprint of an item that originally was published in 1923. How should you transcribe the date in the call number for this item? **1923a—put a lowercase "a" at the end of the date to indicate that it is a facsimile reprint or photocopy.**

5. You are cataloging two editions of the same work published in the same year: 2015. You assign the following call number to one of the editions: NK1170 .B45 2015. What call number should you assign to the other edition to distinguish it from the first? **NK1170 .B45 2015b—put a lowercase "b" at the end of the date to distinguish between editions of the same work published in the same year.**

6. You are cataloging an item that you think was published between 1968 and 1974. How should you transcribe the date in the call number for this item? **1968—transcribe only the earliest year.**

7. You are cataloging an item that was published in either 2001 or 2002. How should you transcribe the date in the call number for this item? **2001—don't put both dates. Choose the earlier date to include at the end of the call number.**

CHAPTER 4: CREATING A MAIN ENTRY CUTTER NUMBER

1. Issa—**.I87**
2. Willis—**.W55**
3. Takachi—**.T35**
4. Anwar—**.A59**
5. Florez—**.F66 (since "l" is between "i" and "o" on line 4, you can choose either "5" or "6" to represent the second letter)**
6. Kyrios—**.K97**
7. Simpson—**.S56**
8. Montgomery—**.M66**
9. MacKenna—**.M33**

10. De Souza—**.D47**
11. Ahrens—**.A37 (since "h" is between "d" and "l–m" on line 1, you can choose either "3" or "4" to represent the second letter)**
12. Chase—**.C53 (since "h" is closer to "i" than it is to "e," I chose "5" to represent "h")**
13. Ko—**.K6 (cannot Cutter any further since the name is only two letters long)**
14. O'Connell—**.O26 (since "c" is between "b" and "d" on line 1, you can choose either "2" or "3" to represent the second letter. Ignore punctuation marks.)**
15. Schmidt—**.S36 ("ch" is treated as one letter on line 2)**
16. *Reference and Information Services*—**.R44**
17. *It's All in Your Head*—**.I87**
18. *Stretching*—**.S77**
19. *The Trickster*—**.T75 (ignore the initial article and Cutter "Trickster")**
20. *On My Own Two Feet*—**.O56 (since "On" is only two letters, keep Cuttering into the next word, "My")**
21. *The Checklist Manifesto*—**.C54**
22. *Quest for the Selby Mirror*—**.Q47 (treat "Qu" as one letter)**

CHAPTER 5: CUTTERS AND THE SHELFLIST

Note: Your answers may not match mine. That's OK. The following is simply one way you can Cutter the names and titles to ensure that they stay in alphabetical order on the shelf.

1. Assume that the authors in the following list have written works on the same topic. Cutter the names in a way that will ensure that they will be in alphabetical order within a shelflist.

   Salmon—**.S25**
   Sanchez—**.S26**
   Santos—**.S268 (Cuttered one digit further in order to distinguish "Santos" from "Sanchez")**
   Saxton—**.S29**

Schofield—**.S36**

Schott—**.S368 (Cuttered one digit further in order to distinguish "Schott" from "Schofield")**

Shah—**.S53**

Short—**.S55**

Silva—**.S56 (I flipped the Cutters for "Short" and "Silva" because otherwise their Cutters would put "Silva" before "Short" on the shelf)**

Simmons—**.S566**

Singh—**.S57 (I modified this one slightly because this one also should be Cuttered .S56. To keep it from getting too long, I simply changed the last digit [6] to 7.)**

2. Assume that the authors in the following list have written works on the same topic. The first two in the list are titles on the same topic. Cutter the names and titles in a way that will ensure that they will be in alphabetical order within a shelflist. If you don't remember what to do with titles that begin with a number, review the last chapter!

3 in a Row (title main entry)—**.A13**

7 Winds Blow (title main entry)—**.A15**

Aaaaa, Bill—**.A23**

Ababa, Pam—**.A233**

Acton, Jill—**.A28**

Adams, Cynthia—**.A33 (Cuttered "Ada")**

Adams, Kathy—**.A336 (Cuttered "Adam")**

Adams, Michael—**.A3367 (Cuttered "Adams")**

Adams, Nancy—**.A33676 (Cuttered "AdamsN")**

Aglow, Thomas—**.A35**

Alfalfa, Charles—**.A44**

CHAPTER 6: LCC IN CLASSIFICATION WEB

1. What three captions are the next step down hierarchically (indented the least) under "Nature photography"? **General works; Plants, flowers, etc.; Animals**

2. What class number should you assign a general work on the nature photography of flowers? **TR724—this is the class number for general works on plants, flowers, etc. (not for nature photography generally, which would be TR721). The work does not have to be about both plants and flowers for it to qualify for TR724— one or the other (or both) is fine.**

3. What other class number does LCC compare to "Nature photography"? **QH46 Pictorial works in natural history—right under the "Nature photography" caption it says: Cf. QH46 Pictorial works in natural history.**

4. Is there a class number associated with just "Animals"? **No, you have to decide if the work you are cataloging is a general work on animal nature photography (TR727) or nature photography of a specific type of animal (TR729.A–Z).**

5. If I have a book of nature photography on an Animal "Special Subject," do I choose TR729.A–Z as my call number? **No, in this context, the "A–Z" after TR729 is a placeholder for the first Cutter, which represents specific animals, such as Birds (.B5) and Elephants (.E45). The use of A–Z is simply LCC's way of saying that your first Cutter should fit alphabetically between A and Z.**

6. If the book in front of you has the LCC number TR729.C69, what is the topic of the book? **Nature photography of cows—don't forget to look at the hierarchy! TR729.C29 is not for works about cows generally, but for works of *nature photography* that feature cows.**

7. What class number should you assign to a book of bark nature photography? **TR726.B3**

CHAPTER 7: BROWSING LCC IN CLASSIFICATION WEB

1. From the main menu of Classification Web, click on Browse LC Classification Schedules and type "BJ66" in the text box next to LC Class #. What is the caption associated with that class number? **General works**

2. Examine the breadcrumbs for the topic in question #1—what is the topic at the beginning of the breadcrumbs? What is a work assigned

BJ66 about? **Ethics; a general work on the study and teaching of ethics or ethics research**

3. Go to the LCC Outline from the main menu of Classification Web and click on L—Education. What is the class number range for "Theory and practice of education"? **LB1–3640**

4. Does the "Theory and practice of education" include the topic of someone's right to education? **No—"Right to education" is covered in LC213, which is outside of the range of "Theory and practice of education" (LB1–3640).**

CHAPTER 8: SEARCHING LCC IN CLASSIFICATION WEB

1. Perform a caption search and then an index search for "Cattle." Find the classification number associated with cattle as air cargo. **HE9788.4.C37**

2. ZA4080 is associated with what topic? **General works on digital libraries**

3. Search for "Apples" using the caption and index search. Which classification number is associated with the food processing of apples? **TP441.A6**

4. Use various search techniques to find the appropriate class number for higher education, specifically focusing on higher education in developing countries. **LC2610**

5. Perform a keyword search for "Phones." What type of phones are in the captions of the search results? **Cell phones**

CHAPTER 9: BASIC LCC CALL NUMBER BUILDING

1. A work on paper-bag cooking by Desmond Quick, published in 1970.

   TX833 .Q53 1970
   MARC: 050 _4 $a TX833 $b .Q53 1970
   Start by searching for the topic "paper-bag cooking" using either the caption or index search (or both). The one search result should be TX833. If you click on TX833, you will see this entry

in the TX schedule, but there is no mention of an additional Cutter needed for this topic. Therefore, Cutter the main entry (Quick = .Q53) and add the publication date (1970).

2. A book of nature photography featuring roses by Roxanne Offerman, published in 1986.

   TR726.R66 O34 1986
   MARC: 050 _4 $a TR726.R66 $b O34 1986
   You can approach this in different ways. You can perform a caption search for "Nature photography," which gives you a range of class numbers: TR721–733. Click on it, and on the first screen you should see "Roses" listed under "Special subjects, A–Z." Additionally, you can perform a keyword search for "nature photography roses," which gives us one result. Either way our class number is TR726, and the first Cutter is .R66, representing "Roses." LCC does not tell us to add any further Cutters, so we can Cutter the main entry, Offerman (O34), and add the publication date (1986).

3. A work on the veterinary anatomy of camels by Tania Fernandez, published in 2012.

   SF767.C28 F47 2012
   MARC: 050 _4 $a SF767.C28 $b F47 2012
   Your search strategy for this work should be similar to the last one. You can either perform a caption search for "veterinary anatomy" or a keyword search for "veterinary anatomy camels" to find the same entry: SF767 for the veterinary anatomy of "Other" animals and .C28 representing camels specifically. Once again, no further Cutters are required within the schedule, so add the main entry Cutter (Fernandez = F47) and the publication date (2012).

4. A work on agricultural structures in New Zealand by Pat Alonso, published in 1983.

   S787.N45 A46 1983
   MARC: 050 _4 $a S787.N45 $b A46 1983

Perform a caption search for "agricultural structures" to receive a range of class numbers: S770–790.3. Since the work is about agricultural structures in New Zealand specifically, we are looking for a class number that allows us to include a geographic place, if possible. When you click on S770–790.3, there are a couple of entries for places, but they are too specific for what we have. If you move forward one page (click on the > button), "By region or country" for agricultural structures begins at S785 with general works on agricultural structures in the United States. New Zealand belongs in "Other regions or countries" (S787), and the first Cutter should represent the region or country (New Zealand = .N45, from the *Classification and Shelflisting Manual* G300). Cutter the main entry next (Alonso = A46) and add the publication date (1983).

5. A work on computer crimes in California by Dorothy Pfeiffer, published in 2001.

   HV6773.23.C2 P44 2001
   MARC: 050 _4 $a HV6773.23.C2 $b P44 2001
   If you perform a caption search for "computer crimes," you receive several results. If you click on each result, the one that fits best is the range HV6772–6773.3, particularly because it allows you to subdivide by geographic area starting at HV6773.2. Since California is a US state, choose HV6773.23 (Computer crimes by region or state), and the first Cutter should represent the state, California (.C2). Next include the Cutter for the main entry, Pfeiffer (P44), and the publication date (2001).

6. A *directory* of landscape architecture in Ohio by Milo Sandyman, published in 1999.

   SB469.34.O3 S26 1999
   MARC: 050 _4 $a SB469.34.O3 $b S26 1999
   An index search works best for finding "landscape architecture" since it does not appear immediately in the caption search result list. But it is the first result in an index search: SB469–476.422. Note how the work is not only about landscape architecture in Ohio, but it is a *directory*. Directories can be organized by region

or country starting at SB469.33. We should choose SB469.34 because this class number is for organizing by US region or state. The first Cutter is for the state, Ohio (.O3), and the second Cutter represents the author, Sandyman (S26). Then add the publication date (1999).

7. A *periodical* on mathematical logic by Declan McSweeny, published in 2016.

   QA9.A1 M43 2016
   MARC: 050 _4 $a QA9.A1 M43 2016
   A caption or index search for "mathematical logic" works well for this one. QA9 represents this topic and .A1 represents "Periodicals, societies, congresses, serial publications" on mathematical logic. This will be our first Cutter. Next, Cutter the main entry, McSweeny (M43), and add the publication date (2016).

8. A general work on the history of dollhouses by Max Schaefer, published in 1990.

   NK4894.A2 S33 1990
   MARC: 050 _4 $a NK4894.A2 $b S33 1990
   Trying to find this topic via caption or index searching is a bit tricky. Our answer lies in the range NK4891.3–4894.4 (Dollhouses: Decorative arts), but that is not obvious from the search result list. If you perform a keyword search for "history dollhouses," the result list is more promising; the first result is NK4894.A2–.2. If you click on it, you can see that general works (indented under History) on the history of dollhouses is NK4894 .A2—this means that .A2 needs to be the first Cutter of our call number after the class number, NK4894. Since our work is not about the history of dollhouses in a specific place, we can add the main entry Cutter (Schaefer = S33) and the publication date (1990).

9. A work on the history of dollhouses in Japan by Hina Ooki, published in 2015.

   NK4894.J3 O65 2015
   MARC: 050 _4 $a NK4894.J3 $b O65 2015

For this one, we can stay on the same page in Classification Web that we were on for the last item. We still have a work on the history of dollhouses, but in a specific country, Japan. LCC says to use NK4894.A3–Z for these works, which means that our first Cutter should represent a region or country *and* be between A3 and Z. Since Japan is Cuttered .J3, it easily fits between A3 and Z. That is our first Cutter; our second Cutter represents the main entry, Ooki (O65), and then add the publication year (2015).

10. A book titled (and about) *An Introduction to Glass Blowing*, edited by Julia Glasbläser (this is a title main entry), probably published in 1968.

    N8217 .G53 I58 1968
    MARC: 050 _4 $a N8217.G53 $b I58 1968
    If you perform a caption search for "glass blowing," you receive one result: N8217.G53. Click on it. The entry for Glass blowing does not specify further Cutters beyond .G53 (representing the special subject: glass blowing). The second Cutter, I58, should *not* represent the editor, Glasbläser, but the title, *Introduction to Glass Blowing*, because this is a title main entry (which is usually the case for edited works). Ignore the initial article ("An") and Cutter "Introduction." Even though this work was "probably" published in 1968, it is fine to put just "1968" rather than add additional characters, such as a question mark or square brackets (see chapter 2 on dates for more information).

CHAPTER 10: ADVANCED CALL
NUMBER BUILDING USING TABLES

1. A history of the information services industry by Shanna Miksa, published in 1997.

    HD9999 .I492 M55 1997
    MARC: 050 _4 $a HD9999.I492 $b M55 1997
    The information services industry is represented by HD9999 .I49–.I494. Click on the hyperlinked "Information services

industry" to apply Table H21. General works about and histories of the information services industry should be classed at HD9999.I492. LCC does not say to add a further Cutter, so Cutter the main entry (Miksa = M55) and add the publication year.

2. A general work on the history of education in Texas by Anna Dover, published in 1980.

LA370 .D68 1980
MARC: 050 _4 $a LA370 $b .D68 1980
Search for "history of education" using the caption or index term search. The second result is for the range LA1–2396. If you move forward several pages, you will encounter the history of education by US state. Next to each state is Table L18, but click on the hyperlinked "Texas"—Classification Web will automatically apply the table to a range of class numbers for Texas (LA370–372). We are cataloging a general work, so LA370 is the best fit. LCC does not say to include a Cutter, so add the Cutter for the author (Dover = .D68) and the publication year (1980).

3. A history of education in Dallas, Texas, by Victor Espino, published in 1995.

LA372 .D3 E87 1995
MARC: 050 _4 $a LA372 .D3 $b E87 1995
This item is a continuation of the last one, but this time our work is about the history of education in a specific city: Dallas, Texas. LA372 allows us to include the city as the first Cutter. Cutter "Dallas" using the LCC Cutter table (D3—you only need to Cutter place names one digit past the initial letter) and then add the main entry Cutter (Espino = E87) and the publication year (1995).

4. A history of railroads in Germany by Felix Zug, published in 2010.

HE3078 .Z84 2010
MARC: 050 _4 $a HE3078 $b .Z84 2010
Table H37 is applied to Germany's range of class numbers (HE3071–3080) when you click on the hyperlinked "Germany." "History" is HE3078, and no Cutters are assigned by LCC (the

Cutter for Germany is not needed because HE3078 can only be applied to works about the history of railroads in Germany). Cutter the main entry, Zug (.Z84), and add the publication year.

5. A general work on private medical care plans in Poland by Ksenia Pawlak, published in 2015.

RA413.5 .P7 P39 2015
MARC: 050 _4 $a RA413.5 .P7 $b P39 2015
RA413.5 represents the topic "private medical care plans, by region or country." It says to subarrange each country by Table R5a. The first Cutter should represent the specific region or country. Click on the hyperlinked "R5a" to see that general works only need the region or country as the first Cutter, but local works require a "2" placed at the end of the first Cutter. Since the work description does not mention that it is about a specific place in Poland, we don't need to worry about Cuttering further by local place. Use the *Classification and Shelflisting Manual* at G300 (https://www.loc.gov/aba/publications/ FreeCSM/G300.pdf) or the Cataloging Calculator to find the Cutter for Poland (.P7), Cutter the author's name (Pawlak = P39), and then add the date of publication (2015).

6. A work on fraud and swindling in Tokyo, Japan, by Ponzi Abagnale, published in 2000.

HV6699 .J32 T63 2000
MARC: 050 _4 $a HV6699 .J32 $b T63 2000
The range of class numbers for "Fraud. Swindling. Confidence games" is HV6691–HV6699. HV6699 is specifically for "Other regions or countries" besides the United States. The caption for HV6699 says to "subarrange each country by Table H73," and if you click on H73, you can see that you can add a "2" to the first Cutter in order to indicate that the second Cutter should represent the local place. The Cutter .J3 is for Japan; add a "2" to it, as I just explained. The second Cutter should be for the local place, Tokyo (T6), plus "3" from line 5 of the Cutter table representing the author, Abagnale (3). Finally, add the date of publication.

7. A work about banana workers in Brazil by Marcos Rocha, published in 2007.

   HD8039.B232 B67 2007
   MARC: 050 _4 $a HD8039.B232 $b B67 2007
   If you search for "banana workers," the result is HD8039.B23–.B232. Click on the hyperlinked "Banana workers" caption to apply Table H50. There are only two options: "General works" and "By region or country." Since this work is about banana workers in Brazil, choose HD8039.B232 (the "2" at the end of the first Cutter indicates that the second Cutter represents the region or country). The Cutter for Brazil is B6. Since we cannot add a third Cutter, use line 5 of the Cutter table to Cutter the first letter of the author's last name (R = 7) and add it to the end of the second Cutter (B67). Then add the year of publication.

8. The work in question 1 translated into Italian, published in 1999.

   HD9999 .I492 M5516 1999
   MARC: 050 _4 $a HD9999.I492 $b M5516 1999
   Find Italian on the Translation Table. The lowercase "x" represents the main entry Cutter (M55). Place "16" at the end of M55 to show that this is an Italian translation of the work. Also make sure you change the year to the publication date of the translation.

9. The work in question 2 translated into Korean, published in 1981.

   LA370 .D68164 1981
   MARC: 050 _4 $a LA370 $b .D68164 1981
   Find Korean on the Translation Table. The lowercase "x" represents the main entry Cutter (D68). Place "164" at the end of D68 to show that this is a Korean translation of the work. Also make sure you change the year to the publication date of the translation.

10. The work in question 3 translated into Arabic, published in 1998.

   LA372 .D3 E87125 1998
   MARC: 050 _4 $a LA372 .D3 $b E87125 1998

Find Arabic on the Translation Table. The lowercase "x" represents the main entry Cutter (E87). Place "125" at the end of E87 to show that this is an Arabic translation of the work. Also make sure you change the year to the publication date of the translation.

11. A polyglot translation of the work in question 4, published in 2014.

    HE3078 .Z8412 2014
    MARC: 050 _4 $a HE3078 $b .Z8412 2014
    Find Polyglot on the Translation Table. The lowercase "x" represents the main entry Cutter (Z84). Place "12" at the end of Z84 to show that this is a Polyglot translation of the work (includes translations in more than two languages). Also make sure you change the year to the publication date of the translation.

12. An autobiography of ice skater Kristi Yamaguchi, published in 2001.

    GV850.Y36 A3 2001
    MARC: 050 _4 $a GV850.Y36 $b A3 2001
    Works on ice skating begin at GV848.9, and biographies of ice skaters are classed at GV850. Use the Biography Table to see that the first Cutter should represent the subject of the autobiography (Yamaguchi = Y36) and the second Cutter (A3) signifies that this is an autobiography. Then add the date of publication, 2001.

13. A biography of physicist Albert Einstein by Emma Grimble, published in 1989.

    QC16.E5 G75 1989
    MARC: 050 _4 $a QC16.E5 $b G75 1989
    If you begin at Physics (QC), you will see that Individual biography begins at QC16 and Einstein has been assigned the Cutter .E5. According to the Biography Table, the second Cutter should represent the main entry, Grimble (G75), and then add the date of publication, 1989.

14. A book of Albert Einstein quotations, published in 1966.

QC16.E5 A25 1966
MARC: 050 _4 $a QC16.E5 $b A25 1966
This one is similar to the last work: it should begin with QC16 .E5, representing Einstein, but the second Cutter represents quotations, which is A25 in the Biography Table (it is included in "Selected Works. Selections"). Then add the publication date, 1966.

15. An interview with rock musician Bruce Springsteen by James Sullivan, published in 1987 (hint: use class number ML420).

ML420.S67 A5 1987
MARC: ML420.S67 $b A5 1987
ML420 represents biographies of singers. According to the Biography Table, Springsteen should be the first Cutter (.S67, though some catalogs use .S77), and the second Cutter should be A5 for interviews. We can ignore the main entry, Sullivan, and add the date of publication, 1987.

CHAPTER 11: ADVANCED CALL NUMBER BUILDING USING EMBEDDED TABLES

1. A general work on art study in universities and colleges in Rhode Island by Arnold King, published in 1983.

N346.R4 K56 1983
MARC: 050 _4 $a N346.R4 $b K56 1983
Since this is a general work on art study in Rhode Island universities and colleges, the first Cutter (represented by "x" in the embedded table) should represent the US state Rhode Island (.R4). Since the table does not specify an additional Cutter, the second Cutter should represent the main entry, King (K56).

2. A work on murder in France, specifically in the city of Paris, by Tristan Guibord, published in 2002. Hint: perform a keyword search for murder by region or country.

HV6535 .F83 P374 2002

MARC: 050 _4 $a HV6535.F83 $b P374 2002

The first Cutter represents France (.F8) plus "3" from the embedded table, which specifies that the second Cutter represents a city (in this case, Paris—P37). Since we cannot add a third Cutter, use line 5 of the Cutter table to change the first letter of the author's name (G) to "4" and add it to the end of the second Cutter.

3. A work on labor productivity in Florida by Agostina Riva, published in 1975.

   HC107 .F63 L37 1975

   050 _4 $a HC107.F63 $b L37 1975

   This one is similar to the example that was worked through in this chapter. Start at HC107. The first Cutter represents the state, Florida (.F6), plus "3" from the embedded table to indicate that the second Cutter will represent a special topic (in this case, labor productivity). The embedded table says to go to HC79 to find the topic; "labor productivity" is L3. Since we cannot add another Cutter for the author, Riva, use line 5 of the Cutter table to Cutter the first letter of the last name (R = 7) and place it at the end of the second Cutter. Finally, add the publication date (1975).

4. A work on planetariums in Phoenix, Arizona, by Gina Stargazer, probably published in 1942.

   QB71 .U62 P57 1942

   MARC: 050 _4 $a QB71.U62 $b P57 1942

   QB71 represents works on planetariums by region or country. The first Cutter represents the United States (.U6) plus a "2" from the embedded table to indicate that the second Cutter should represent individual planetariums by city. The second Cutter is composed of Phoenix (P5) and the author, Stargazer (S = 7 on line 5 of the Cutter table). Even though the work was "probably" published in 1942, we can just put "1942" in the call number without additional qualifications (see chapter 2 on dates).

5. The study and teaching of dairying in Dairyland, Wisconsin, by Tom Leche, published in 1989.

SF243.5 .W62 D355 1989
MARC: 050 _4 $a SF243.5 .W62 $b D355 1989
SF243.5 represents works about the study and teaching or research of dairy cattle by US region or state. Since this work is about study and teaching in a particular city, Dairyland in Wisconsin, use the Local, A–Z in the embedded table. The first Cutter represents the US state Wisconsin (.W6), and then add "2" to the end of that Cutter to show that the second Cutter will represent a local place in Wisconsin: Dairyland (D35). Since this does not leave room for the author, Leche, use line 5 of the Cutter table to Cutter the first letter of the author's last name (L = 5). Place the "5" at the end of the second Cutter; then add the publication date.

CHAPTER 12: CLASSIFYING FICTION IN LCC

1. *The Jungle Book*, a novel by British author Rudyard Kipling, published in 1965.

PR4854.J8 1965
MARC: 050 _4 $a PR4854 $b .J8 1965
Perform a caption search for "Kipling, Rudyard" and choose the literature result: his range of class numbers is at PR4850– 4858. His entry says "Table P–PZ33 modified," but don't let that throw you off. Click on his name and a table you are familiar with appears. Notice the entries in yellow. This is the "modified" part of Table P–PZ33 that you can use if your institution has a very large collection of Kipling's works. Otherwise, the "nonmodified" Table P–PZ33 is sufficient. Regardless, we have a separate title, *The Jungle Book*, and not a collected work. Separate titles are at PR4854.A–Z and organized by title. You are given the option to subarrange the separate titles by Table P–PZ43, but our book is not a translation, selection, or criticism, so we can ignore it. The first Cutter should

be the title; skip the "The" and Cutter "Jungle" (.J8). Then add the publication date, 1965.

2. *Sphere*, a novel by American author Michael Crichton, published in 1999.

PS3553 .R48 S6 1999
MARC: 050 _4 $a PS3553.R48 $b S6 1999
Perform a caption search for "Crichton, Michael" and click on PS3553.R48. Click on his name to incorporate Table P–PZ40. Since the work in hand is a separate work, focus on PS3553 .R48A61–.R48Z458. PS3553.R48 begins the call number, then Cutter the title (Sphere = S6). Add the publication date, 1999.

3. *The Grass Is Singing*, a novel by British author Doris Lessing, published in 2008.

PR6023 .E833 G7 2008
MARC: 050 _4 $a PR6023.E833 $b G7 2008
Perform a caption search for "Lessing, Doris" and choose the literature result: PR6023.E833. Click on her name to incorporate Table P–PZ40. Since the work in hand is a separate work, focus on PR6023.E833A61–.E833Z458. PR6023.E833 begins the call number, then Cutter the title (skip the "The" and Cutter "Grass"): G7. Add the publication date, 2008.

4. *Americana*, a novel by American author Don DeLillo, published in 1989.

PS3554 .E4425 A62 1989
MARC: 050 _4 $a PS3554.E4425 $b A62 1989
Perform a caption search for "DeLillo, Don" and this is the result: PS3554.E4425. Click on it and then on DeLillo's hyperlinked name to apply Table P–PZ40. Since *Americana* is a separate work, we need to focus on this: PS3554.E4425A61– .E4425Z458 (Separate works. By title). This one is a little tricky because if we Cutter *Americana* to only one digit past the initial letter, we get A4. This is problematic because A4 does *not* fit between A61 and Z458, the Cutter range for separate works by DeLillo. A4 is reserved for German translations of separate or

collected works by DeLillo. The best option for this work is to adjust the Cutter for *Americana* to A61 or A62, the beginning of the separate works range of Cutters. I chose A62 just in case we need to use A61 for some other work published in the future titled something alphabetically before *Americana*.

5. *Stardust*, a novel by British American author Neil Gaiman, published in 1997.

PR6057 .A319 S7 1997
MARC: 050 _4 $a PR6057.A319 $b S7 1997
Neil Gaiman is not listed in Classification Web when you search for him, so find his authority record in LC Authorities (http://authorities.loc.gov). According to his authority record, the Library of Congress uses PR6057.A319 for Gaiman. P–PZ40 is the typical table used for fiction works, and it tells us that separate works should be organized by title. Cutter the title, *Stardust* (S7), and add the publication date.

6. *Ficciones*, the selected works of Argentinean author Jorge Luis Borges, edited by Huberto Rubio, published in 1962.

PQ7797 .B635 A6 1962
MARC: 050 _4 $a PQ7797.B635 $b A6 1962
Perform a caption search for "Borges, Jorge Luis" and you receive two results: PN6071.B72 (collections of literature *about* Borges) and PQ7797.B635 (works by Borges within Spanish literature, specifically Argentina). Choose PQ7797.B635 and click on Borges's name to incorporate Table P–PZ40. Since *Ficciones* is Borges's selected works, choose PQ7797.B635A6, which is "Selected works. Selections. By date." Add the publication date, 1962. The description does not say, but if this was a translation of the original Spanish work, then we would choose PQ7797.B635 A199 through A59, depending on the translation (for example, A2 for an English translation) and then add the publication date.

7. The collected works of Lewis Carroll (pseudonym of Charles Lutwidge Dodgson), published in 1951 (no editor given).

PR4611 .A1 1951

MARC: 050 _4 $a PR4611 $b .A1 1951

This one is tricky because Lewis Carroll is listed under his real name, Charles Lutwidge Dodgson, but the caption does have Lewis Carroll in it. A keyword search for Lewis Carroll gets you there, as well as looking at his authority record. Carroll's works are at PR4611–4612. Table P–PZ36 is applied when you click on his name. Since this is a collection of his works, we have two options: PR4611.A1 for collected works by date and PR4611.A2 for collected works by editor (if given). Since the editor is *not* given, use PR4611.A1, add the publication date, and you are done!

CHAPTER 13: OTHER AVENUES AND RESOURCES

1. Which LCC number is associated with the LCSH "Digital cameras"? **TR256**
2. Which LCC number is associated with the LCSH "Linked data"? **Z666.73.L56**
3. What range of LCC numbers should you use for works on dude ranches? **GV198.945–975**
4. LCSH "Apples" is associated with which LCC numbers? **QK495 .R78 (Botany) and SB363–363.6 (Culture)**
5. You are cataloging a work on "Tea," but the focus is on tea customs. If you look up "Tea" in LCSH, which LCC numbers are associated with tea customs? **GT2905–2916**
6. Is there an LCC number associated with the LCSH "Trees—Identification"? If not, what other ways can we determine an LCC number for this topic other than searching directly in LCC? **One way is to use the Bibliographic Correlations tool within Classification Web (accessible via the home page of Classification Web). Type "Trees—Identification" and then search LC subject heading → LC class number. You will receive multiple class numbers from records in the Library of Congress's catalog. Another way is to search OCLC's Classify service (http://classify.oclc.org/clas sify2). Search "Trees—Identification" as a FAST subject head-**

ing and you can click on the results to see what LCC numbers are assigned to the works associated with this topic.

7. Use the Bibliographic Correlations tool to find the most common LCC number used with the following LCSHs:

   a. Unicorns **GR830.U6**

   b. Timing circuits **TK7868.T5**

   c. Dating (Social customs) **HQ801**

   d. Cats—Behavior **SF446.5**

   e. Impressionism (Art)—France **ND547.5.I4**

Regions and Countries Table (G300)
(courtesy of Library of Congress)

Iceland I2
India I4
Indochina I48
Indonesia I5
Inner Mongolia *see* China
Iran I7
Iraq I72
Ireland I73
Islamic countries I74
Islamic Empire I742
Islands of the Indian Ocean I743
Israel I75
Italy I8
Ivory Coast *see* Côte d'Ivoire
Jamaica J25
Japan J3
Java *see* Indonesia
Jerusalem J4
Jordan J6
Jugoslavia *see* Yugoslavia
Jutland *see* Denmark
Kampuchea *see* Cambodia
Kazakhstan K3
Kenya K4
Kerguelen Islands K43
Kiribati K5
Korea K6
Korea (Democratic People's Republic) *see* Korea (North)
Korea (North) K7
Korea (Republic) *see* Korea
Korea (South) *see* Korea
Kosovo K8
Kuwait K9
Kyrgyzstan K98
Laos L28
Latin America L29
Latvia L35

US States and Canadian Provinces Table (G302) (courtesy of Library of Congress)

U.S. STATES

CANADIAN PROVINCES

Glossary

Alphanumeric: notation or codes containing both numbers and letters. Library of Congress class numbers contain both numbers and letters (HD8039), and Dewey Decimal class numbers contain only numbers (352). Cutters are also alphanumeric.

Captions: within the LCC schedules, these present the meaning of a class number using English words.

Classification (or Class) Number: the alphanumeric notation at the beginning of an LCC call number that represents primarily the main topic of a work, but sometimes represents other things, like the author of a fiction work. Each class number is divided into subclasses.

Cutter(s): alphanumeric codes designed to organize an item alphabetically within a topic, usually by the main access point (i.e., the author's last name or the title of the book), but sometimes by geographic area or special topic as well. Named after their inventor, Charles A. Cutter.

Cutter Numbers: see Cutter(s).

Cutter Table: table used to construct Cutters. The one used in this book is more specifically the Library of Congress Classification Cutter Table. There are other Cutter tables (such as the Cutter-Sanborn Table) that are used with other classification schemes.

Embedded Tables: tables included as part of the schedule text that allow the call number creator to build more specific LCC call numbers at certain class numbers.

Geographic Cutters: Cutters that represent a geographic place, like a country, region, or US state.

Main Entry Cutters: Cutters representing either the main (or first-listed) author or the title if there is no main author of a work.

Notation: characters that make up a class or subclass.

Schedules: the notation, terminology, and instructions for each class.

Shelflist: the inventory of a library's resources as they are ordered on the library's shelves.

Table(s): lists of notations that you can use to further build a call number. Tables can either be embedded in the schedule text at a particular class number or they can be accessed separately and used across multiple class numbers.

Work Letter: a lowercase letter placed at the end of the date in a call number to either distinguish call numbers that would otherwise look identical (same topic, same author, same publication date) or to distinguish between an original work and a facsimile reprint of that same work.

Index

About the Author

Karen Snow is an associate professor in the School of Information Studies at Dominican University in River Forest, Illinois. She teaches face to face and online in the areas of cataloging, classification, and metadata. She completed her PhD in information science at the University of North Texas in 2011 and while doing so worked as a cataloger in the Rare Book Room, the University Archives, and the Technical Services Department. She taught several cataloging courses online for the College of Information at the University of North Texas from 2006 until 2011. Her main areas of research interest are cataloging quality, ethics, and education. In 2016, she received the Follett Corporation's Excellence in Teaching Award.